Relativism
in the Arts

Relativism
in the Arts

Edited by
Betty Jean Craige

The University
of Georgia Press
Athens

Copyright © 1983 by the University of Georgia Press
Athens, Georgia 30602
"The Two Relativisms: Point of View and Indeterminacy in the Novel *Absalom, Absalom!*" copyright
© 1983 by J. Hillis Miller.

Set in 11 on 14 Linotron 202 Electra

The paper in this book meets the guidelines for per-
manence and durability of the Committee on Production Guidelines for Book Longevity of the
Council on Library Resources.
Printed in the United States of America.

Library of Congress Cataloging in Publication Data
Main entry under title:

Relativism in the arts.

    Contents: What is relativism in the arts? / Betty
Jean Craige — The appreciation and interpretation
of works of art / Arthur Danto — The limits of relativism in the arts / Hayden White — [etc.]
    1. Arts—Philosophy—Addresses, essays, lectures.
    2. Arts, Modern—20th century—Addresses, es-
says, lectures.   3. Relativity—Addresses, essays,
lectures.   I. Craige, Betty Jean.
BH301.R43R44   700'.1   82-4726
ISBN 0-8203-0625-8   AACR2

I like to think in my more Hegelian moments that the purpose of art is to make the philosophy of art possible.

Arthur C. Danto

Contents

Relativism
in the Arts

Betty Jean Craige

What is Relativism in the Arts?

Possession [1]

Oh immensity! Within your multiplications there is
only I, that am not I but rather just the subject
of that language that is usually called human.
The unthinkable is pronounced, the incredible is calculated,
it suddenly appears to us that we are dominant
when we are subject to the object clamoring
that it does not, not ever, fit within our ideas
vociferous only. We are the voice of no one.
We are never we but rather that other in us
possessed by the nothingness of the delirious no one.

Gabriel Celaya

For the Spanish poet Gabriel Celaya, the implication for man
of the relativistic universe—the universe without center, without fixed frame of reference, where time and space form a
continuum—is finally the acknowledgment that the "self,"
the concept of the individual (as a spiritual-intellectual, non-
material, entity) definable independently of environment, is but
a construct of Western philosophy, dependent upon the self/
world (subject/object, spirit/matter) dualism that in turn depends
upon a fixed frame of reference, a centered universe. In our late
twentieth-century self-consciousness of the role of language in
shaping thought, we can see, as Celaya says, that whereas we
once thought the "I" to be subject *of* the verb, in charge of the

language it uses to express "itself," the "I" is actually dependent upon that language, subject *to* (that is, governed by) language. The thoughts the "I" pronounces are thoughts made possible by the linguistic-epistemic system of the thinker—in fact, brought into being to a great extent by that system. Now the "I" confronts its own disappearance, which is to say that the "I"—itself the "voice of no *one*"—acknowledges that it never actually had a self. The twentieth-century relativist "I" is self-deconstructing. So the humanist concept of man, dependent upon the spirit/ matter opposition of a universe with a God, will disappear, for which reason Foucault announced that the death of God is the death of "man."[2]

The relativity associated with Einstein's map of the universe extends itself into all domains of our culture's exploration of the world. Einstein's notion that point of view determines the appearance of physical phenomena makes itself felt in history and in psychology, as well as in literature; and Heisenberg's notion that the process (or method) of observation determines our definition of the object of observation calls into question the belief in the possibility of empirical objectivity for any discipline. In short, the accepted theories of modern physics undermine the Cartesian belief in the separation of subject and object by which the self had stood in the privileged position of observer of an external, objectively definable material reality. The shift to the relativist paradigm occurring in the twentieth century manifests itself in the arts in the rejection of representation, which is in turn a rejection of the privileged position of the artist-as-creator in charge of his art to express him-self and to re-present an "external reality." Avant-garde artists are now illustrating this transition from humanism to post-humanism.

What is implied in the avant-garde artists' rejection of representationalism? What aesthetic expressions of humanism do they find inappropriate for relativism? The humanism and its accompanying dualism that made the self so important, and finally so isolated, in the period from the seventeenth century through the early twentieth century produced the artist (poet, novelist, painter, composer) who assumed his work to be psychologically an expression of himself—that is, an externalization of his own thoughts about that presumed objectively definable material reality or about himself—and legally his own property. Humanism, with its emphasis on the accurate observation of nature, ultimately provided for the development of modern history as description of external events, the development of the novel as imitation history, the realist aesthetic in the visual arts, and empiricism in science.

In painting, humanism produced the fixed perspective. For the artist to achieve on his canvas a representation of the world as it appeared visually to him, he had to be conscious of his position in relation to the objects he was painting. And by maintaining his fixed position, or perspective, he could paint "realistically": he could re-present, apparently objectively, an external material reality because he believed he was separate from it. Paradoxically, however, this consciousness of fixed perspective and vanishing point did not become a metaphysical self-consciousness about the process of observation until the late nineteenth century: the subjectivism implicit in the fixed perspective masqueraded as impartial observation, or objectivity, because every human being apprehends the world from a single point of view, that of his own eyes, and experiences a separation from the object of his vision. The same principle operated in the novel during this period. The novelist, imitating the historian, could describe a sequence of fictive events "realistically" by assuming that he, like the historian, was capable of impartial observation of an external reality. In effect, the realist novelist himself maintained a fixed perspective (even when entering the subjectivity of one character after another) by unconsciously organizing and valorizing the fictive phenomena according to his own order of things, which, to the extent that his culture considered his novel to be realistic, was his culture's order of things. Such a fixed perspective served to establish what Barthes has called the "single 'theological' meaning (the 'message' of the Author-God)" which the traditional reader sought in the traditional (dualist) text.[3] The realist novelist wrote with the presupposition of a centered universe in which objects, persons, and events had fixed, intrinsic meaning, as did his own text.

The perceived separation of observer from observed rested in turn upon another presupposition, that of the neutrality of language. As long as language remained invisible, a presumably neutral medium for the transmission of thoughts, man could believe in the possibility of objective description. Not until man became conscious of the function of the observer's point of view in his understanding and description of the world did language become visible; and suddenly, in the face of this now non-transparent, non-neutral symbolic system which governs our organization and valorization of phenomena, twentieth-century man shifts his focus from an external reality to the process by which he apprehends phenomena. For us, the object of our observation has become our very process of observing, which we now see to be ordered by our language. The twentieth-century relativist accepts not only Einstein's theory of relativity but also Benjamin Lee Whorf's, which holds that "all observers are not led by the same physical evidence to the same picture of the universe, unless their linguistic backgrounds are similar, or can in some way be calibrated."[4]

The foregrounding of language as a "prisonhouse" (Nietzsche) leads to the collapse of our belief in the autonomy of author, text, and reader. When the author discloses himself to be constructed by the linguistic-epistemic system in which he is writing, then the text discloses itself to be a construct of "multiple writings, drawn from many cultures and entering into mutual relations of dialogue, parody, contestation," and the reader becomes "the space on which all the quotations that make up a writing are inscribed without any of them being lost," as Roland Barthes says.[5] If language is not a neutral vehicle for the poet's communication of an idea, neither is it a neutral vehicle for the reader's apprehension of that idea: for just as many voices speak in the consciousness of the poet, governing his writing, so do many (other) voices speak in the consciousness of the reader, governing his reading. The reader can no longer think of himself as a neutral receiver of the meaning intrinsic to the particular configuration of words comprising the poem; he must now acknowledge that he participates in the creation of its meaning and that every reader reads ("[re]writes," as Barthes would say) the poem in a different way. So the poem has no fixed, intrinsic meaning.

If this is so, then no artwork has a fixed, intrinsic meaning. Every artwork must acquire its meaning relative to its observer, who becomes a creator of its meaning—but within, of course, the constraints upon him of various systems: for example, with respect to the visual arts, the constraints are those of the artworld, museums, the discipline of art history within the universities, the contemporary conventions of understanding artworks, and his own education. The observer structured by these institutions apprehends not only the artworks of the present but also all those of the past with the eyes of his own age; and, as T. S. Eliot said in "Tradition and the Individual Talent," his awareness of the entry of a new artwork into the artworld changes the meaning of all past artworks. Meaning is contextual.

The recognition of this relativity of meaning presents itself in many twentieth-century avant-garde artworks in which the artist dramatizes a self-negation, or rather an abandonment of his traditional role of controlling the meaning of his work. In the early decades of our century various writers, painters, and composers rebelled against artistic conventions by rejecting the fixed perspective—by rejecting omniscient ("realist") narration, representational painting, musical tonality. Eliot in *The Waste Land* juxtaposed the cultural "fragments" we have inherited to show the constitution of the twentieth-century mind, the mind of a culture that had loosed itself from its roots. By not providing explicit connections between the fragments or a traditional climactic order for them so as to make one fragment serve as center from which the others would obtain their value, Eliot (hypothetically) transferred to the reader the responsibility for giving order and meaning to the poem. And although the reader does not invent its meaning, since he reads with the expectations and conventions of his culture's literary history, he becomes conscious of his own role as participant in the poem's construction. Picasso rejected the realist aesthetic with its fixed perspective in *Les Demoiselles d'Avignon* and thus refused to allow his painting to serve the spectator as an invisible window through which to see a reality outside it; he forced the spectator to become conscious of the painting as a painting, in and of itself. And Stravinsky rejected tonality in *The Rite of Spring*, establishing his own ad hoc rules for apprehending the work. Eliot, Picasso, and Stravinsky all rejected the presupposition of an external, fixed frame of reference when they rejected conventional modes of constructing their artworks; instead, they established their own frames of reference within the particular works, presenting a relativist aesthetic.

Other artists have gone beyond Eliot, Picasso, and Stravinsky to bring into focus the audience's role in the creation and definition of the artwork. Marcel Duchamp's entry of a urinal entitled *Fountain* in the Independents Exhibition of 1917 called into question the Western definition of art as "precious" by calling into question the role of the artist as creator of the artwork; it thus foregrounded the role of the artworld, of the community, in the establishment of what a given epoch defines as art. His gesture served to state for the artworld that "meaning is contextual."

The artist Hans Haacke has more recently created "invisible art" in his *Rain Tree*, which drips water in patterns, and *Sky Line*, a nylon line supported by hundreds of helium-filled white balloons.[6] Jim Dine has created a happening called *Vaudeville Act* which he has described in this way: "I came out with a red suit on and cotton all over me, my face painted yellow. To the music that was going on, I pulled the cotton off and just let it fall to the floor until there was no cotton on me. Then I walked out."[7] Donald Burgy has created a conceptual art "piece" consisting of statements only, as follows:

Name Idea No. I

Observe something as it changes in time. Record its names.
Observe something as it changes in scale. Record its names.
Observe something as it changes in hierarchy. Record its names.
Observe something as it changes in differentiation. Record its names.
Observe something as it changes under different emotions. Record its names.
Observe something as it changes in different languages. Record its names.
Observe something which never changes. Record its names.[8]

By creating artworks that seem to those outside the artworld to be merely "real things," these artists have revealed as conventional the distinction held since Plato between "art" and "non-art," a distinction dependent upon the form/content dualism that makes art representational. In her article "Against Interpretation" Susan Sontag argued that all Western consciousness of and reflection upon art have remained within the confines staked out by the Greek theory of art as mimesis or representation. It is through this theory that art as such—above and beyond given works of art—becomes problematic, in need of defense. And it is the defense of art which gives birth to the odd vision by which something we have learned to call "form" is separated off from something we have learned to call "content," and to the well-intentioned move which makes content essential and form accessory.[9]

When the twentieth century turns its attention to language and sees language as governing the conception of phenomena which a given culture may have, then the form/content distinction vanishes. Art ceases to have mimesis or representation as its primary motivation in the absence of that dualism; consequently, its definition becomes problematic. How can we distinguish art from non-art if art does not attempt to represent something other than itself? How can we distinguish art from non-art if the *form* of the artwork is its *content*? And how can we distinguish art from non-art if, in a decentered universe, phenomena lack intrinsic significance—that is, if significance discloses itself to be manmade, relative to culture and time period? These questions arising from the recognition that a culture's discourse establishes the shape of its reality—and that therefore discourse is both form and content—lead to the institutional theory of art outlined by George Dickie. According to that theory, "The institutional structure in which the art object is embedded, not different kinds of appreciation, makes the difference between the appreciation of art and the appreciation of nonart."[10] For Arthur Danto, interpretations constitute artworks, and there are no artworks without interpretations. Meaning is therefore contextual for both Dickie and Danto, as it must be in a world without a transcendental signified to provide a stop to the endless process of signification.

Those artists challenging the aesthetic conventions of mimesis, the conventions determining the development of Western art, have forced us to turn our attention to the institutions that define art, and in so doing they relegate the actual art object to a position secondary to the concept they wish to present by that artwork. Art becomes "conceptual" when it ceases to be representational. One could argue that conceptual art is indeed symbolic, since it represents an idea, but I would maintain that such "representation" differs from that of traditional art in that the conceptual art object itself is empty of transcendent significance. Duchamp's urinal, unlike Michelangelo's *Pietà*, has not even an illusory intrinsic aesthetic value.

Stanley Fish makes an argument parallel to Dickie's when he declares that there is no such thing as "ordinary language," since "at its heart is precisely that realm of values, intentions, and purposes which is often assumed to be the exclusive property of literature." This erasure of the traditional distinction between poetic language and ordinary language raises a question: What is literature? To that Fish replies: "It is language around which we have drawn a frame, a frame that indicates a decision to regard with a particular self-consciousness the resources language has always possessed."[11] So we must turn our attention to our process of framing, to the institutions which provide the frames, to our conventions of reading (and seeing and listening), to our own discourse.

When we focus on our discourse as the source of the presuppositions, values, and ideas for our poetry, painting, and music, we remove the aura from both the artwork and the artist. The artwork becomes an object of no transcendent value (since nothing has transcendent value in the relativist paradigm) whose meaning depends upon its context, which includes the artworld and the observer; and the artist becomes "the voice of no one," possessed by his language and by the voices of his culture's past.

When we focus on our own discourse, no longer believing either in an objectively definable external reality or in our-selves as isolable entities capable of impartial observation or original thought, we gaze upon our own process of making order. We gaze upon this process of making order with eyes—with minds— constructed by that very process. We are relativists born of the relativist paradigm, believing in a relativist order of things in which the meaning of phenomena appears manmade relative to culture and epoch; yet, as relativists, we must also acknowledge that the relativism we see in our twentieth-century reality must be in some way the relativism we impose upon it in the order we give to events. Our relativist minds made by a relativist world make a relativist world. And there is no Truth in us.

The relativist's assertion that there is no Truth, no "transcendental signified," as Derrida puts it,[12] has produced not only an outpouring of theoretical writings on the implications of the death of God for the field of aesthetics but also a hostile reaction on the part of those traditional critics who do not accept relativity in fields other than physics. The battle between the two sides— between those who accept the decentered universe and see as its necessary correlative the decentered artwork, and those who may or may not accept the decentered universe but do not see art and criticism as necessarily reflecting such a universe—has been occasionally quite bitter, since no less than the meaning of everything is at stake. The recognition that we are involved in what we see has inspired art that focuses on its own making (on its medium, on its physical status, on its apprehension by the beholder/listener/reader), criticism that focuses on itself as creative of the artwork, and aesthetic theory that moves beyond its traditional boundaries into the fields of sociology, anthropology, linguistics, psychoanalysis, and philosophy to examine man's process of giving order to phenomena. The mission of these avant-garde artists, critics, and theorists is the systematic deconstruction of "logocentrism" (Derrida's expression for the undue privilege that Western culture at least since Plato has accorded to forms of discourse purporting to mirror an "external reality"; the belief that the word is carrier of an absolute value). It is the rejection of the goal of representation.

Yet not everyone involved in the arts has taken on the task of dramatizing a breakdown in the self/world dualism that gave the artwork intrinsic meaning and gave the critic the role of discovering that meaning. The essays collected here represent a variety of responses to twentieth-century relativism, out of which these issues grow. Anna Balakian, who refuses Barthes' proclamation of the death of the author and the corresponding death of the critic, outlines in her contribution the consequences (which she rejects) of relativist theory for practical criticism. Describing as "creative criticism" that discussion of a text which issues from the (ex)critic's assumption that the reader constructs the text's "meaning," Balakian argues that the critic (not dead, for her) is *not* an artist but instead an intermediary creating "a bridge between two distinct aspects of human cognizance." In order to perform this function, she says, "the critic has to be also something of a moralist; i.e., must possess an a priori code of values against which he tests the *fiction* of the creative artist and recasts it in terms of identifiable and differentiable components in regard to pre-established norms shared by the non-artists." In her effort to save the critic from his dissolution in a world of relative values, Balakian is also trying to save the artwork, arguing against Arthur Danto's thesis that "an object is an artwork at all only in relation to an interpretation." She holds to an absolute distinction between art and non-art, one which depends on the belief in the "life" of the author, who is the artwork's "god," spelling out "its values, its hierarchy, the relative functions within an integrated whole, satisfying his own and his readers' holistic yearnings." Balakian continues the theological metaphor in defining the artwork itself as "sacred," "a system of symbolization of which the correspondences are strictly intramural or self-referential to start and become intermural only when other artists accept the signal-making character of the work."

Balakian's belief that the author (not dead) creates a symbolic self-sustaining work whose meaning is intrinsic and which can therefore be discovered by a critic depends upon the dualism that the relativist critics (and artists) attempt to prove illusory. Two theoreticians who present definitions of art which they find to be compatible with a *non*-dualist understanding of reality (and who in one way or another oppose Balakian) are Hayden White and Arthur Danto. Both accept the relativist proposition that, in White's words, "objects do not have essential natures [and therefore] the only possible meaning or value they might possess would be that which inheres in their relationships with other objects," but White seeks the definition of art in the process of its making (its use as symbol) whereas Danto seeks the definition of art in the process of its reception (its interpretation). White says that his resistance to radical relativism in the arts "may be the result of a residual religiosity or idealism in our secularist thinking, but it is also an intuition of the kind of value that human beings are able to produce by the kind of symbolizing labor that we can *see* went into the production of certain kinds of commodities as against others." The artwork calls attention to itself as such by inducing in its beholders a "self-consciousness about the symbolizing process of which it is an instantiation." To explain how Duchamp's *Fountain*, which was not created for symbolic use by a manufacturer of urinals, acquires status as an artwork, White argues that Duchamp's entry of it in the exhibition was a "symbolizing gesture" and therefore creative.

Danto also discusses the importance of Duchamp's gesture for

for twentieth-century aesthetics, as it required philosophers of
art to seek a theory of art that would account for artworks that
were also "real things." In accord with the general twentieth-
century redirecting of attention from an external reality to our
own process of perceiving, our process of making order, Danto
shifts his attention from the art object to the culture's process of
making meaning, which is interpretation. For him, interpretation "transforms objects into works of art," and it may turn *any*
object into a work of art. Yet Danto maintains that there may be
misinterpretation, and that, because artworks are constituted by
interpretation, "works are misconstituted when interpretation is
wrong." The relativism resulting from the recognition of a decentered universe does not imply that all interpretations of phenomena are equally valid; and in the artworld the "possible
interpretations are constrained by the artist's location in the
world, by when and where he lived, by what experiences he
could have had."

Thus both Danto and White, like Balakian, consider intention to be at least partly constitutive of the work's meaning,
although Balakian imagines an ahistorical relation between author, text, and reader, whereas Danto and White see intention
to be historical, governed by social, political, psychological, and
linguistic systems operating in the culture at the time of the
artist's construction of his work. Yet all three would argue that
the artist's intention, problematical as it may be, constitutes a
constraint upon the possible appropriate meanings the beholder/
listener/reader may construct in his apprehension of the work,
and both Danto and White use Duchamp's *Fountain* as a test
for the usefulness of their theories to account for twentieth-
century art. In effect, Duchamp forced philosophers of art into
what Wellek and Warren called "extrinsic criticism" of the artwork by dramatizing the function of the artworld in defining the

art of a given epoch: he dramatized the implications of a decentered universe with no transcendental signified to provide transcendental significance for the artwork.

Yet Duchamp's gesture did something else for twentieth-century art: it demonstrated that, if the artwork has no intrinsic meaning, it is in effect a philosophical statement. When the dualist believed that form held content (whose meaning was fixed and transcendent), he could look through the form of the (precious) artwork to glimpse and interpret that content—to reveal the meaning of Michaelangelo's *Pietà*, Beethoven's Ninth Symphony, Goethe's *Faust*; but when the relativist loses this belief, he looks to the form, for form is everything. And form reveals the human process of making order. So Duchamp's gesture of presenting what we could call a "self-evacuating artifact" (with apologies to Stanley Fish) signals the participation of artists in the culture-wide self-reflectivity occasioned by the loss of belief in intrinsic meaning.

This self-reflectivity in particular artworks is the subject of the articles by Elliott Schwartz, Donald Kuspit, J. Hillis Miller, and Ronald Bogue, all of whom investigate how twentieth-century works of music, painting, and literature turn back upon themselves to focus on the process of their making. Schwartz says that contemporary musical composers are now "*consciously* aware" of the function in performance of space (physical, architectural, acoustical), the objects occupying that space (musical instruments, human bodies, chairs), the ritual of the performance (the behavior of the musicians, the behavior of the audience in relation to the musicians on stage or in a part), and the illusion (the possibility of music to evoke various emotions, or to recall various events). Just as the traditional distinction between art (all the arts) and philosophy disappears when art becomes conceptual, so does the distinction between music and drama disappear when the musician calls attention to the form of the performance. Schwartz describes one of his own pieces, *Elevator Music*, with "the audience in a moving elevator, the players in vestibules outside the elevator doors," as a composition dramatizing the function of the environment on the reception of the particular work. The effect is also to desanctify the work: such a piece does not exist in a realm removed from the profane reality of "real things," for it is indeed a "real thing." Yet paradoxically, by being a "real thing" *Elevator Music* serves to make a philosophical statement about its own status as a musical composition in a world that has traditionally believed the work to be, in Balakian's words, "a system of symbolization of which the correspondences are strictly intramural or self-referential to start."

Donald Kuspit analyzes the collage as a form of art in which "we find abstract elements as material fragments—elements of a code of abstraction that no longer perform the abstractive function, but exist as entities in their own right." By exhibiting "real things" (such as pieces of newspaper or string) as constituting its physical existence within its frame, the collage argues against the aesthetic of representationalism, by which the painting served to present the illusion of its being a window onto something beyond it. The collage calls attention to its own making as a physical object whose content is its form, and in so doing it desanctifies itself: nothing is sacred in a world where we recognize that content is form, that human reality takes the shape that our linguistic system and social practices give it.

Narrative, too, exhibits the process of its own construction in the avant-garde novels of our century. J. Hillis Miller and Ronald Bogue, informed by the theoretical work of Derrida and Foucault, examine novels by Faulkner and Robbe-Grillet as relativist texts revealing the function of language in the making of human reality. Miller discusses *Absalom, Absalom!* as a text exhibiting the inevitable failure of language to capture "reality," to tell the "truth" about events, and the human necessity to pursue this goal of mimesis, this goal of "getting the story right." For Miller, Faulkner's novel demonstrates "the fact that all narrative is in one way or another a figure for something which cannot be adequately figured, much less adequately named in straightforward referential language." Faulkner thus anticipates Derrida, who argues that there is always a surplus of signification, a "*super-abundance* of the signifier" that is "the result of a lack which must be *supplemented*."[13] This lack is what makes all narratives doomed to failure.

Robbe-Grillet's acknowledgment of this lack, which becomes subject to discussion and to illustration in the twentieth century when the prisonhouse of language comes into view, appears in his novels that formally frustrate the reader's attempt to use the structure of words to create a coherent sequence of events independent of their narration. Whereas Faulkner illustrated that lack thematically and structurally *within* his novel, in the relationship of his characters to the unnameable past and in their recognition of the failure of language to get the story right, Robbe-Grillet illustrates it in the relationship of the novel to its reader: he forces the reader to look at the text itself as a structure of words. In an examination of all of Robbe-Grillet's fiction, Bogue points out the various devices by which Robbe-Grillet undermines the reader's traditional belief in the mimetic function of narrative. In *La Maison de rendez-vous* and the novels written thereafter, Robbe-Grillet creates characters that, says Bogue, are not "trans-textual": he breaks up time to allow no recuperation of a coherent chronology for the events described; he deforms space to make a textual space that "is purely its own, subsumable within no human perspective—whether objective, subjective, or oneiric." Finally, Robbe-Grillet dramatizes the death of the author, which Bogue relates to Foucault's pronouncement of the death of man, by making visible, particularly in *Project for a*

Revolution in New York and *Topology of a Phantom City*, the process of generating the text. And the generators (whether words, letters, colors, pictures), Robbe-Grillet states, are materials supplied by the social world, not creations of an autonomous imagination. The exposure of the author's process of generating his text, like the exposure of the collage artist's gathering of his materials, removes not only the illusion of representation but also the illusion of the artist as invisible creator of a fictive world. So the author reveals himself to be constructed by the interacting social, linguistic, psychological, and political systems of his culture.

By deconstructing himself as author, Robbe-Grillet accomplishes in his fiction what Celaya asserts in his poem: the "I" that Western culture has for five hundred years assumed to be an isolable self capable of original thought is "the voice of no one." This assertion is, finally, the challenge of relativism to Western humanism that disturbs the most; and, in the field of aesthetics, it threatens the whole enterprise of criticism. When the artist disappears as an original thinker, his work likewise disappears as a repository for his thoughts; and when that happens, then the activity of interpretation (the disclosing of the meaning within the form) becomes gratuitous. So the "death of man" which disturbs all humanists is the "death of the author" which disturbs all critics, for the "death of the author" is, as Barthes says, the "death of the critic." [14] As the relativism in the air of the twentieth century has produced relativism in the arts—in the artworks themselves—relativism in the arts may call into being a new kind of discourse about artworks, one which will perhaps not be directed toward "interpretation."

Perhaps. Or perhaps it will call into being a new kind of interpretation, one that becomes possible for the critic (reborn) who has learned from relativism that, as Fish says, "interpretation is the only game in town."[15] We can never *not* interpret. The critics who may once have committed suicide to enter the paradise of metacriticism may now be the "ghosts that returned to earth" to hear the large red man read (in Wallace Stevens's poem) "from the poem of life," "those that would have wept to step barefoot into reality."[16] For while we talk of the author's losing his authority as a creator, while we talk of the text as "made of multiple writings," while we talk of the reader as "the space on which all the quotations that make up a writing are inscribed," artists are at work on poems, plays, novels, paintings, sculptures, and compositions that pique our curiosity. If we believe that the art of an age reflects its paradigm—that relativism in the arts, for example, reflects relativism in the twentieth-century mind—then we shall be *compelled* to seek the possible meanings of our artworks, for we are driven to interpret. Yet our recognition that meaning is manmade, a recognition which disturbed the existentialists, may finally relieve us of the anxiety of "getting the story right." J. Hillis Miller's "interpretation" of *Absalom, Absalom!*, made possible by his understanding of the issues of contemporary philosophy and literary theory, made possible by his acceptance of relativism, should reassure Anna Balakian that the critic is not dead. He has returned from "the wilderness of stars" to touch "the most coiled thorn," the artwork that holds not the secret of its creator but of its culture, the artwork whose meaning is not single and divine but plural and of this world. It is of the earth, that most coiled thorn, but that is enough for the relativist.

Notes

1. La posesión

   ¡Oh inmensidad!, nada hay dentro de tus multiplicaciones
   salvo yo que no soy yo sino tan sólo el sujeto
   de ese leguaje que suele decirse que es humano.

Se pronuncia lo impensable, se calcula lo increíble,
nos parece de repente que somos dominantes
cuando somos lo sujeto por el objeto clamante
que no, no, no cabe nunca dentro de nuestras ideas
sólo vociferantes. Somos la voz de nadie.
No somos nunca nosotros sino lo otro en nosotros
poseídos por la nada del nadie delirante.

From Gabriel Celaya, *Poesía Hoy* (Madrid: Espasa-Calpe, S.A., 1981), pp. 182–83. My translation.

2. Michel Foucault, *The Order of Things* (New York: Random House, 1970), pp. 385–86. Foucault says, "Since man was constituted at a time when language was doomed to dispersion, will he not be dispersed when language regains its unity?"

3. See Roland Barthes, "The Death of the Author," in *Image, Music, Text*, trans. Stephen Heath (New York: Hill and Wang, 1977), p. 146. Barthes says, "We know now that a text is not a line of words releasing a single 'theological' meaning (the 'message' of the Author-God) but a multi-dimensional space in which a variety of writings, none of them original, blend and clash. The text is a tissue of quotations drawn from the innumerable centres of culture."

4. Benjamin Lee Whorf, *Language, Thought, and Reality* (Cambridge: MIT Press, 1956), p. 214.

5. Barthes, "Death of the Author," p. 148.

6. The artwork is described by Jack Burnham in *Great Western Salt Works* (New York: George Braziller, 1974), p. 22.

7. Michael Kirby, *Happenings* (New York: Dutton, 1965), p. 186.

8. Ursula Meyer, *Conceptual Art* (New York: Dutton, 1972), p. 90.

9. Susan Sontag, *Against Interpretation* (New York: Dell, 1966), p. 4.

10. George Dickie, *Art and the Aesthetic: An Institutional Analysis* (Ithaca: Cornell University Press, 1974), p. 41.

11. Stanley Fish, *Is There a Text in This Class?* (Cambridge: Harvard University Press, 1980), pp. 108–9.

12. See Jacques Derrida, "Structure, Sign, and Play in the Discourse of the Human Sciences," in *The Structuralist Controversy*, ed. Richard Macksey and Eugenio Donato (Baltimore: Johns Hopkins University Press, 1970), pp. 247–65. Derrida writes: "From then

on it was probably necessary to begin to think that there was no center, that the center could not be thought in the form of a being-present, that the center had no natural locus, that it was not a fixed locus but a function, a sort of non-locus in which an infinite number of sign-substitutions came into play. This moment was that in which language invaded the universal problematic; that in which, in the absence of a center or origin, everything became discourse—provided we can agree on this word—that is to say, when everything became a system where the central signified, the original or transcendental signified, is never absolutely present outside a system of differences. The absence of the transcendental signified extends the domain and the interplay of signification *ad infinitum*" (p. 249).

13. Ibid., p. 262.
14. See Barthes, "Death of the Author," pp. 142–48. Barthes says: "Once the Author is removed, the claim to decipher a text becomes quite futile. To give a text an Author is to impose a limit on that text, to furnish it with a final signified, to close the writing. Such a conception suits criticism very well, the latter then allotting itself the important task of discovering the Author (or its hypostases: society, history, psyche, liberty) beneath the work: when the Author has been found, the text is 'explained'—victory to the critic. Hence there is no surprise in the fact that, historically, the reign of the Author has also been that of the Critic, nor again in the fact that criticism (be it new) is today undermined along with the Author" (p. 147).
15. Fish, *Is There a Text*, p. 355.
16. Wallace Stevens, *The Collected Poems of Wallace Stevens* (New York: Alfred A. Knopf, 1971), pp. 423–24.

Arthur C. Danto   **The Appreciation
and Interpretation
of Works of Art**

Genius, according to Schopenhauer, is the capacity for knowing
the Ideas of things—in the Platonic sense of Ideas—and for revealing these Ideas in works of art for the benefit of the remainder of mankind who, borrowing as it were the eyes of genius,
may behold through these works what the genius beholds directly. "The work of art is only a means for facilitating this knowledge," Schopenhauer writes, treating art as a cognitive prosthetic,
a metaphysical window through which we may view the deeper
realities but which has no further cognitive contribution of its
own to make. It is to be seen through, but not itself to be seen—
the more transparent, the better. Accordingly, aesthetic response
is to be elicited not directly by the work of art, which aspires to a
kind of nothingness, but by what the work of art discloses or (as
the aestheticians of the eighteenth century would have said) *dis-
covers* or (since we are being historical, as Heidegger would say)
unconceals. As the work of art is really only what it is of, Schopenhauer feels justified in saying that "aesthetic pleasure is one
and the same, whether called for by a work of art or directly by
the contemplation of life and nature."

The ideal of the self-diaphanizing artwork is very ancient. It
is, for example, a fantasy of the mimetic theory of art that the
work of art should present to eye or ear only what would have
been presented to them by the object imitated. As such, presen-

tation underdetermines the distinction between reality and art, to which it is invariant, and illusion becomes not only a possibility but also a goal. The gauzy essence of art is perhaps enshrined in the wider concept of the *medium*, that which sacrifices its own identity that an Other should be made present through it. In the spiritualistic parlor the departed soul communicates through the medium, gone symbolically unconscious. In the concert hall the performer acts as a kind of medium through which the music is made audible. (A pianist of obviously extraordinary gifts was recently disqualified from the Chopin competition on the grounds that his flashy playing occluded the music it was his task to make present.) On the theatrical stage the highest art of acting is no evident acting at all, as when the audience becomes conscious not of Proust's Berma, but instead of Phédre herself, to the end of whose enfleshment Berma had the uncanny knack of disappearing as herself. (In a recent autobiography the British actor Alec McGowen recalls having gotten too many laughs in his role as Hadrian VII, concluding that it was the performance rather than the role, contrary to the requirements of serious comedy, that amused his audience.)

Art, in this view, aims exactly at the sort of nothingness Sartre supposes consciousness to exemplify, as it is ontologically disqualified to be an object, at least for itself; or which Berkeley speaks of as spirituality, in the respect that spirits are never present to themselves as their ideas are—they can form no idea of themselves because they are, instead, the media through which ideas are given. Since it is not an object unless it falls short of its intentions, the fact that it is an artwork is to play no role of its own in provoking aesthetic responses. Those responses are only to what the medium contains—the "content"—and are the same whether the content is confronted directly, as by Schopenhauer's genius, or as a *pis-aller* through a glass clearly.

It is possible to appreciate the recent history of art as a philosophical effort to reassert its own identity, to infuse itself with the space which theory had required it to vacate, to clot that emptiness and spurn the thin rewards of mediumhood by drawing attention to itself, sometimes brashly: to become "a reality," as artists are fond of saying. And one stratagem for achieving this has been more or less to turn the tables on reality by forcing undeniably real objects to serve as media, possessing them like spooks, so that the works of such masters of reverse artistic magic as Marcel Duchamp present themselves in the bodies of objects we would have no way of knowing were not snowshovels or bottle racks, bicycle wheels or grooming combs. But perfect embodiment, like perfect transparency, seems, ironically, to leave the work of art as weightless as ever. What have we here to respond to, save the snowshovel itself, however possessed? And Schopenhauer's contention that aesthetic pleasure is one and the same appears to have an even greater claim to consideration, for artwork and crass object are as indiscernible as two crass objects of the same unedifying type. It is comical how little difference it seems to make whether art is an airy nothing revealing reality in its nakedness, or so gluts itself with reality that between reality and itself there is no visible difference.

Imagine three altogether similar snowshovels, all from the same factory, one of which is definitely a work of art, though not to be told apart from its vastly less illustrious peers by protracted and minute inspection—not least of all because, though an artwork, it remains also what it has been all along, an outdoor tool of seasonal use. The question of the nature of art arises with this "also," for what, apart from and in addition to its identity as a snowshovel, does it "also" have which makes it an ontological companion of *L'Embarquement à l'île de Cythère* or *Tristan und Isolde*? And can the fact that it is an artwork ("also") make any aesthetic difference? If aesthetic response is always and only to what meets the eye (or ear or whatever other sense), it is difficult to see where aesthetic difference can lie, given the indiscriminability of our snowshovels. If there is a difference, it must lie logically hidden from the senses in what remains when we subtract snowshovel from artwork. Locating this remnant is like seeking the soul by subtracting the body from the person when it is not clear that there *is* a remainder. In the case of works of art, it is difficult to see what "aesthetic response" could amount to, if it is to be a response to something so singularly impalpable.

I nevertheless wish to argue that Schopenhauer is wrong, and that the fact that something is an artwork makes an aesthetic difference, even if that artwork is not to be told apart from a mere thing like a snowshovel. And this means that the work of art cannot be identified either with the *néant* of mimetic eva-nescence nor with the *être* of Duchampian achievement: Being and Nothingness cannot exhaust the metaphysical plane if works of art are to have a locus on it. Aesthetically speaking, the two comically interlocked theories of art are equivalent. So I shall use the possibility of aesthetic difference to prepare the stage, which has been dominated by comedians who merely inter-change masks, for another sort of theory altogether.

That another sort of theory altogether is required may be gath-ered from the fact that both theories just caricatured give us the same thing as subject for aesthetic predicates, and neither can in consequence be adequate to what we may term the "language of the artworld." That this has not, until now, been gathered may be explained by the fact that the concept of beauty has domi-nated aesthetic discussion down through the ages. That fixation has blinded philosophers to the richness of this language and has concealed from them its logic. The "Transparency theory" of art withdraws from aesthetic consideration, of course, every-thing except the content of the work, the rest not bearing on art's essence. The "Reality theory" withdraws from art everything except the reality which would be the content of the artwork as construed by the Transparency theory. So any aesthetic predicates apply to that invariant thing, whatever it may be. To be sure, it would hardly have occurred to the artists of Schopenhauer's time to have revealed an Idea so contaminated with *Alltäglichkeit* as a snowshovel, the lessons of caravaggism not having been thought through to their limit. So let us take some flowers. Aesthetically speaking, it matters little whether it is a diaphanized representation of flowers, or a bunch of flowers elevated by the Flower Artist, who uses daffodils as her material, into a work of art, or *just* a bunch of flowers. Aesthetically, the differences are inscrutable. A beautiful representation of flowers is just a representation of beautiful flowers, as the Transparency theory gives us nothing but the content of the work to serve as subject for aesthetic prediction. And let us grant that the flowers are beautiful, whether they are those taken up into the artworld by the Flower Artist using the zero degree of artistic intervention, or those, otherwise exactly like them, that she happens not to have left deliberately untouched. These were touched by Ellen Williams, a very nice woman but not an artist, and certainly not the Flower Artist. They are beautiful in their sameness, irrespective of ontology.

The Transparency theory gives a formula for creating beautiful works of art: "Pick a beautiful object and represent it with maximum transparency." Such was the formula of the ancient Greeks, as Lessing characterizes them in *Laocoön*: "The wise Greek confined painting strictly to the imitation of beauty: the Greek artist imitated nothing that was not beautiful." The Reality theory abbreviates the creative procedures radically, its formula being, "Pick a beautiful object and let it be a work of art." The aesthetic theory in either case is this: If the subject of the work is F, for any aesthetic predicate F, the work will be F if suitably transparent. And here is the trouble with the concept of beauty. Things in the world—say, flowers—can be beautiful in ways which do not make puzzling, much less conspicuously nonsensical, the inference from beautiful paintings of x's to paintings of beautiful x's. The moment we avert our eyes from beauty and survey the wider resources of our aesthetic vocabulary, however, we may begin to have doubts about this inference even in the case of beauty. I am thinking just now of some powerful drawings of flowers I would resist describing as drawings of powerful flowers. I would resist it because I am uncertain whether there are any powerful flowers, and because I am certain that, if there are any, these snapdragons and irises are not they. "Powerful" is a commonplace item in the language of the artworld, but in fact there is scarcely a predicate of ordinary discourse which cannot be pressed into aesthetic service. So there are fluid drawings and clunky drawings, fragile drawings and witty drawings, explosive drawings and childlike drawings of flowers which, even in the most likely cases, are probably not fragile according to anything like the same criteria that drawings of them are fragile. It is not my intention here to elaborate the logic of these predicates, or their psychology. I want only to say that there must be some subject for them which neither of the theories considered can identify, and to draw out a few philosophical lessons before proceeding to my main preoccupations.

As long as philosophical attention was fixated on the concept of beauty, it was possible to speculate that there might be a *sense* of beauty, through the avenue of which the aesthetical qualities of things would be conveyed to consciousness—just as we become conscious of the colors of things through the visual sense. From the sensibility theorists of the Enlightenment to the Bloomsbury intuitionists, the idea that aesthetic appreciation presupposed some sort of *Anschauung* was allowed by the concept of beauty to be more or less taken for granted. But there could hardly be a temptation to postulate a special sense for each of the aesthetic predicates—a sense of powerfulness, or fragility, or clunkiness. Moral vocabulary is also rich and varied, but it was possible to suppose that goodness entered into the definition of every such predicate, and that goodness itself was, as it were, intuited by a special moral sense. It is unlikely that a parallel theory is available for beauty, and in general it seems to me that one consequence of merely noting the extensiveness of the aesthetic vocabulary is to diminish the attractiveness of the sensation model for aesthetic understanding. Indeed, aesthetic understanding of works of art may be far closer to an intellectual action than to a mode of sensory stimulation or passion, at least when dealing with works of art.

It is perhaps unclear whether the sorts of aesthetic predicates I am referring to apply under the same criteria to works of art and to mere real things when the latter are addressed aesthetically. It is a fact that flowers are fragile, and their fragility, which is factual, has made flowers natural metaphors for fading insubstantialities elsewhere in the world: for physical beauty, innocence, virtue, youth, and happiness. Cherry blossoms in Japan occasion thoughts of the fleetingness of life: but then we are viewing these showers of pink and white petals under the framework afforded by a kind of philosophy of life and treating them virtually from the perspectives of art. Abstracted from these metaphorical and philosophical impulses, would the fragility of flowers ever become a matter of aesthetic focus? Enjoined to heed the fragility of flowers, I take this either as an injunction to watch my clumsy step or to see them as the subject of a poem. Ernst Gombrich's clever remark that we *see* what we paint is not, really, a thesis about optics, but a thesis about the manner in which theories about life and the world affect the way we respond to the world. So when someone says (as Marx Wartofsky has done) that El Greco has enabled him to see the elongatedness of things, treating El Greco as an optical revelator, he is overlooking the possibility that elongation is the artistic expression of the opposed tension between earth and heaven that his stretched saints metaphorically exhibit. In fact, it is possible to argue that the language of the artworld is metaphoric in its semantics. True, this may mean that Schopenhauer's thesis stands—that aesthetic response is the same, whether to artworks or to real things. But this will be because real things are seen under the perspective of art when responded to aesthetically. So we can save the thesis only by rotating it 180 degrees. To be sure, this leaves the concept of beauty to be dealt with, if this is the one main concept to which the distinction between nature and art—at least when art is explained through either of the theories here canvassed—is indifferent. But then we are left with a curious question: What, save the predicates of beauty, could have formed the critical discourse of the ancients? Their experience of art must have been singularly impoverished relative to our own if all they could say was, "How beautiful!" To be sure, they could also praise artworks for their transparency; viz., the grapes he painted looked good enough to eat, the woman he carved looked soft enough to love, etc.

Finally, we may note the irrelevance of aesthetic considerations to the deep problems of the philosophy of art. Those problems have to do with answering the question our trio of snowshovels raises, namely, how to distinguish the one that is art from the one that is not. If Schopenhauer is right, the aesthetic qualities are of a piece as between art and reality, and we can hardly distinguish things on the basis of what they have in common. If he is wrong, then the fact that something is an artwork makes an aesthetic difference. But the aesthetic difference presupposes the distinction we are after and cannot be part of what makes that difference. So aesthetics does not pertain to the essence of art—which does not mean that we won't learn something about aesthetics from identifying that essence. Back to our snowshovels!

The snowshovel which "also" is an artwork suitably bears a title—in this instance, *In Advance of the Broken Arm,* at first glance one of Duchamp's lamer jokes. But then one comes to see that no one is going to break his (or her?) arm shoveling snow with *In Advance of the Broken Arm,* because its promotion to the status of art lifts it above (or at any rate outside) the domain of the mere utensil. So there is a tension after all between work of art and tool which the title wittily underlines. An important subgenre of Duchamp's oeuvre may be appreciated as so many wry comments on a dark thesis of Kant's, according to which art is to be viewed in terms of a generalized purposefulness which yet cannot be identified with any specific purpose. The question of its use is always legitimate, though no answer is allowed as correct. Duchamp shows us tools stripped of their usefulness by their uncomfortable new status, *Zuhandene* thrust into the domain of *Vorhandene,* to use Heidegger's political metaphor, as out of place as a plumber at an April-in-Paris ball. Duchamp makes the metaphysical homelessness of these objects vivid and even intoxicating—but then, surely, appreciation of these works must consist in part in feeling the philosophical tensions they give rise to, rather than, as it were, mooning over their Significant Forms or whatever. It would be an ironic and irrelevant fact, for instance, if the ratio of diameter to height in Warhol's *Campbell's Soup Can* happened exactly to satisfy the golden section!

Consider in this respect Duchamp's celebrated *Fountain* (1917), which, as everyone knows, was but a urinal of that period disconnected from the plumbing which gives it its familiar utility (familiar, at least, to just under half the population of the West) and turned on its back like an immobilized turtle. It is a piece of industrial porcelain, purchased by Duchamp (himself!) from among undistinguished look-alikes produced by a company called Mott Works. It is inconsistent with the spirit of the work to imagine Duchamp anxiously examining the urinals in the salesplace until he found "just the right one." Indeed, the original has been lost (it exists only in a famous photograph taken by Alfred Stieglitz), but Duchamp purchased another one for the Sidney Janis Gallery and a third for the Galleria Schwartz in Milan, and in fact subsequently put out an edition of eight, signed and numbered, as though he had issued an edition of etchings. The signature is Duchamp's, but the name—"R. Mutt"— is not, though, as we know, Duchamp gave himself various names for various other subgenres of his output; e.g., "Rrose Selavy" for his erotica. The difference between name and signature may have struck the artworld of his time as odder than it would today, when one of the main loci of graffiti, aside from subway cars, is men's rooms; and it is a convention that executants of this form of art conceal their identity under special *noms de crayon*, splashed on in a manner no less than in a form that little distinguishes "R. Mutt 1917" from "Taki 191" or "Zorbo 219," save the extra digit. Its being a signature, of course, goes with its being a work of art, a status acknowledged by the Hanging Committee of the Independents Exhibition of 1917 who *rejected* it—you don't reject *things* from art shows; you *exclude* them. Of course, the designer of that urinal, proud of his work, might have signed it—artisans, after all, also sign their productions, as collectors of antiques know. But the crudeness with which "R. Mutt 1917" is splashed on is inconsistent with pride of artisanship. It is a perfectly elegant bit of ceramics, but its elegance is scarcely relevant to appreciating the artwork, of which the signature, which cannot here be separated from the work, is as inelegant as can be. So it should be plain that Duchamp was not redeeming for aesthetic delectation an object up to then deemed crass beyond consideration, a reminder, say, that beauty is to be found in the least likely places. But the grip of aestheticism on the philosophy of art is strong and cold, as may be gathered from the fact that the aesthetic qualities of the urinal are taken to be what *Fountain* is all about in the view of George Dickie, the institutionalist theoretician of art who partially defines art in terms of its candidacy for appreciation. Aesthetic appreciation must be what is meant if his defense of this theory is to make sense. "Why," Dickie asks, "cannot the ordinary qualities of *Fountain*—its gleaming white surface, the depth revealed when it reflects images or surrounding objects, its pleasing oval shape—be appreciated? It has qualities similar to those of works by Brancusi and Moore, which many do not balk at saying they appreciate." These *are* qualities of the urinal in question, as they are qualities of all those heavy-duty numbers from Mott Works in that era. And these *are* qualities in part shared by that part of Brancusi's *Bird in Space*, which itself was classed as an industrial product by a sensitive customs inspector. As a matter of art-historical fact, we know that Duchamp seized upon his ready-mades precisely because they were, in his view, aesthetically indifferent. One of these, a metal comb with the dumb title "Comb"—or perhaps not so dumb, since the literal reading of it would cause us to overlook a neatly inscribed nonsense phrase (*Trois ou quatre gouttes de hauteur n'ont rien à voir avec la sauvagerie*) along its spine—possesses what Duchamp identifies as "the characteristics of the true ready-made": "During the 48 years since it was chosen as a ready-made this little iron comb had kept the characteristics of the true ready-made: No beauty, no ugliness, nothing particularly aesthetic about it . . . it was not even stolen in all those 48 years!"

Professor Ted Cohen has claimed that *Fountain* is not the uri-

nal at all, but the gesture of exhibiting it: and gestures lack sur-
faces, whether gleaming or dull. Cohen thus locates *Fountain*
in the genre of the happening rather than (as would be my in-
clination) as a contribution to the history of sculpture. To be
sure, an argument is available that sculptors can shape events as
well as matter, and function in time as well as in space. But the
existence of duplicates and replicas goes counter to this classification—it is not the gesture of exhibition which is duplicated,
but the urinal, together with whatever makes it art. Moreover,
the gesture of exhibition, which is witty and daring and brash, is
not in the spirit of the ready-made, which is supposed to be
dull. So the work is rather more conservative than Cohen supposes. That such a theory as Cohen's is available at all, however,
is evidence that the identity of the work is pretty indeterminate
even now, after sixty-five years. As different aesthetic qualities go
with the various interpretations—Dickie's white radiance, Cohen's audacity—it is difficult to know what to appreciate until
we know how the work is to be interpreted.

The anonymous defender of *Fountain* in the second issue of
the fly-by-night journal *The Blind Man*—not coincidentally
published by Duchamp himself, among others—writes thus:
"Mr. Mutt . . . took an ordinary article of life, placed it so that
its useful significance disappeared under the new title and point
of view—created a new thought for that object." The "thought"
must concern the power of titles to exsubstantiate objects as resistant to sublation as urinals must be, considering that it is the
urinal which remains the object of critical consciousness to this
very day, and so it is not clear that the power in question extends quite that far. What we have is the giddy spectacle of a
concept—the concept of art—which has bitten off more than it
can chew, like a hapless python with an unswallowable lump in
its suddenly inadequate gullet. It could be a metaphor for art's
ultimate resistance to being ingested by its own philosophy. In

any case, what "Mr. Mutt" is claimed to have created is a *new* thought for *that* object: so the work must be thought *cum* object, taken together, and the object accordingly, is only *part* of the work. The object *may* indeed have those qualities singled out by Dickie, without it following that the work *must* have them. And so appreciation remains in suspense, pending the outcome of interpreting.

Fountain is not to every art lover's taste, and I confess that, much as I admire it philosophically, I should, were it given to me, exchange it as quickly as I could for virtually any Chardin or Morandi—or even, given the exaggerations of the art market, for a middling chateau in the Loire valley. But this has nothing to do with my taste for glistening white porcelain, which I greatly prefer to the decorator colors found in middle-class johns across the continent, as being somehow more "classic." But for just these reasons I find, and I think anyone sharing my tastes would find, something repulsive in the smeary "R. Mutt 1917," which would send me quickly to the Ajax can and Brillo box. Taste, after all, has its inconsistencies, even if it is relative and the paradigm of what cannot be rationally disputed. So let us ponder the inadvertent vandalism of someone who scours off that hideous lettering, thinking it to be graffiti, in order to stand back and vibrate to the arctic sublimities of Mott Works' finest, responding aesthetically to an object pure in curvature and colorlessness, a bare bit of beauty fit for Euclid's cold eye, perhaps a joy forever. Under so exalted a perspective it ought not to matter where or when the object was made, or even that it was made by human intervention, for it is possible to imagine the right combination of kaolin, feldspar, and quartz, shaped and fired in the bowels of the earth at 700 to 800 degrees Fahrenheit, and discovered by Bouvard and Pecuchet, who donate it to the Natural History Museum, while its counterpart, this time by virtue

of a historical rather than a geological counterfactual, lies across
the Marie-Theresian Platz, where it was brought as artistic booty
by the victorious Austro-Hungarians in 1918 and placed in the
Kunsthistorische Museum next to the Breughels. What an inspired curatorial choice, considering that Flemish master's well-
known penchant for urinary wit!

Purity of response goes with purity of object, which means, I
suppose, the object purified of any historical or cultural associations. So the muttless object could have any number of histories,
for all our aestheticism decrees. Alas, Vienna lacks an Oriental
museum, but we can perhaps imagine Prince Eugene of Savoy
prevailed upon to build one in order to house one of the prizes.
The Chinese were the finest ceramicists known, and I can imagine them having produced circa A.D. 1000 an object just like
ours, made deliberately perforated to render it conspicuously
useless for the residual purposes of Chinese porcelain, whose
paradigmatic exemplars would be jars and pots, in order to emphasize that *this* was intended *only* for contemplation by those
responsive to the white mists and waterfalls of the Sung, and to
emblemize the Neo-Confucian teaching that works of art are to
be treated as ends withal, and never as means. It is easy to fit the
identical object—identical at least under one-place predicates,
whether these have primary, secondary, or (as some aestheticians
suppose) tertiary properties as their extensions—into different
contexts. In each context we in fact—if the object is in that context an artwork, as it is in two of those just laid out—respond to
something which is not presented to the senses, not even aug-
mented by the sense of beauty. But let us suppose that lesson
understood, and focus for analytical purposes on those properties which do present themselves to the senses, and on some of
which the eye (for instance) may dwell just for the pleasure it
thereby derives.

Suppose choices are made for purely aesthetic reasons, where by "purely aesthetic reasons" I mean that these are choices of what we simply prefer, without having been taught to prefer it, and without further reasons for preference. Johannes Kepler, had he had his way with the universe, would have preferred circular to elliptical orbits for his planets, because he had internalized a set of metaphysical reasons which mandated circular motion as somehow the most perfect sort of motion. Ellipses seemed unworthy of a universe designed by a Perfect Being. The physicist James Rainwater won the Nobel Prize in physics for his suggestion that certain puzzling properties of the nucleus would follow as a matter of course if the nucleus were shaped like a cigar—an ignominious form, because of whose ignominy Rainwater's conjecture met resistance. Scientists were convinced (and this in 1978!), for who knows what deep reasons, that the nucleus had to be a *sphere*. As with shapes, so with colors. White is a metaphor for purity and "because of its purity" is preferable to scarlet, which connects the choice to background imperatives in the religious unconscious. Scarlet is the hue of sin (if we suppress the thought of cardinal robes), doubtless because it is the color of fire, and fire is, for reasons which, if not obvious, will never be found out, a metaphor for anger and sexual passion. And so on. But there are choices made by animals at the operant level which have to be explained aesthetically, without their aesthetics being explained by their beliefs: there are things which dogs and cats like, smells and tastes, just because they do like them. There may be causes in the DNA material, without the animal having reasons. These would then be pure aesthetic choices. I expect we make them too.

Writing on the topic of boredom, with which some of his work is associated, Andy Warhol writes that it is important to sit and watch the same thing. "I don't want it to be essentially the same, I want it to be exactly the same. Because the more you look at the same exact thing, the more the meaning goes away and the better and emptier you feel." This sounds about like a formula for contemplation, where any sufficiently dull object— a doorknob, one's own navel—is a means for attaining that good empty feeling Warhol's fellow mystics tend to pursue. But I wish to stress the disappearance of meaning, leaving the bare object, even if, living as we do in intensionalized, situational-ized worlds, it is far from plain that very much aesthetically will remain when meaning is subtracted. In any case, it would only be after such subtraction that the object which remains would give rise in us to what I am calling *pure* aesthetic responses. Now taste, as a matter of conceptual truth, is relative, even if in fact everyone always prefers the same thing. And so suppose that it is established by psychologists and anthropologists, working as they do with neonates, exotic tribes, total amnesiacs, and hydro-cephalics, that there is a universal spontaneous aesthetic prefer-ence for just the object Duchamp happens to have chosen for *Fountain*, invariably as to questions of meaning and background metaphysics. He has discovered the Universal Aesthetic Object! After all, there has to be some reason why the designer at Mott Works chose that modified trifoil over the countless forms avail-able for much the same function. All this is meant to get us as close as possible to an aesthetic tabula rasa, and my only pur-pose is to show that nothing remotely like this is available for *Fountain* itself, as an artwork, regardless of whatever delight the object it is materially related to may bring to the uncontami-nated seventh sense of newborn babes and bushmen. It would not be possible to experiment with neonates regarding *Foun-tain*'s identity as a work of art, for while they may have an over-whelming, irresistible propensity for contemplating *that object*, they are conceptually innocent of what an artwork is. There is something to which the neonate is blind that the critic of *Blind Man* could see—namely, that, whatever it is, which is not merely adjoined to the seductive form of worldwide charm, but which may in fact cause that form to go under: to "disappear." It is not even clear what color *Fountain* is, or if it has a color. It is at this, rather than at what we can nakedly aestheticize, that we must look to see what an artwork is. And it will call for a very different sort of aesthetic from what pure aesthetic responses exemplify.

Indiscernible objects become, or can become, quite different and distinct works of art by dint of distinct and different interpretations, so I shall think of interpretations as functions which transform material objects into works of art. Interpretation is, in effect, the lever with which an object is lifted out of the real world and into the artworld, where it becomes vested in often unexpected raiment. Only in relation to an interpretation is a material object an artwork, which of course does not entail that what is an artwork is relative in any further interesting way. The artwork a thing becomes may, in fact, have a remarkable stability.

It perhaps goes without saying that not every artwork is a transformation through an interpretation of an *objet trouvé*. With most works of art it takes some trouble to imagine counterparts (as with our triad of snowshovels) which are not works of art, chiefly because most artworks are objects thrust into the world with the intention that they be works of art. Still, as I hope I have shown, here as elsewhere, it is always possible to imagine something indiscernible from an artwork but caused in a way which renders a transformative interpretation inapplicable. This does not mean that the object is beyond redemption—it can be interpreted into arthood—but it could scarcely be the work we have in mind when we imagine this new but perfectly congruent thing. Suppose, as a cultural terrorist, I decide to blow up the marble quarries at Carrara, to make a statement once and for all regarding the politico-moral corruption of the Renaissance. I plant tons of plastic explosive and depress the detonator with a song of anarchy on my lips. The dust clears, and there, in the midst of it all, the lumps of marble have fallen together to form what could not be told apart from the *Tempietto* of Bramante—except for the fact that it is topped by what cannot be told apart from the *Pietà with Saint Nicodemus* of Michelangelo. That sculpture would be radically out of place atop that exquisite structure, an adorable architectural metaphor whereby a Roman templum is transfigured into an emblem of Roman Christianity, and historical continuity as well as religious triumph is celebrated through monumental reference. But this curiously shaped hunk of marble is no more out of place atop this pile of marble lumps than anything else would be. Rather, there is no room here for the concept of place: we have only a statistically odd jumble of rock, fallen where and as it has fallen; external similarities notwithstanding, there is nothing here of reference or metaphor. Not that jumbles cannot be metaphors; only that this isn't. Of course, it could be a miracle, a benign bit of meddling on the part of the spirit of Pope Julius II. But it could not mean what the *Tempietto* of Bramante means, even if I convert on the spot. So though an artist might have planted all that plastic and detonated it in the hope that something *just like this* would happen, I am uncertain what work he has produced. I seek interpretation, but it won't be the interpretation which gives the *Tempietto* its locus in the history of Renaissance architecture.

The concept of art gives rise to two sorts of mistakes, one philosophical and the other merely critical. The first is interpreting something which is not in candidacy for art, and the second consists in giving the wrong interpretation of the right sort of thing. I may go through the motions of interpreting the snow-shovel, only to discover that I have interpreted the wrong one—which is different from discovering that I have given the wrong interpretation of the proper object. There are views of artistic interpretation in which, while it may be correct or incorrect to interpret a given object, there is no correct or incorrect interpretation. You have yours; I have mine. I shall now explore enough of the logic of artistic interpretation to imply a view on this extreme sort of relativism.

The fourteenth edition of the *Encyclopædia Britannica* defines fountains as arrangements for letting water gush into an ornamental basin, as well as, one may suppose through metonymy, the ornamental receptacle or "the jet of water itself." Mott Works' urinal fits this definition. Had Duchamp been bent on lexicographical mischief, he would have put the definers to some labor to exclude this unwelcome newcomer from the range of the definiendum because of slackness in the definiens. I think his intentions were less to get urinals classed as fountains, which would make his title into a label, than to leave its connotations intact as a civilized device for relieving cystic distension, and to thrust it metaphorically under the attributes of fountains as works of sculptural architecture. Those works encompass such achievements as the Schönen Brunnen of Nuremburg, the Fontana di Trevi in Rome, the Fontaine des Innocents by Jean Gujon in Paris, Paul Manship's Prometheus Fountain in Rockefeller Plaza, and not least of all the *Mannequin Pisse* of the sculptor Duquesnoy in Brussels, upon which, to show how mores may have changed between 1619 and 1917, Louis XV is said to have conferred the coveted Croix de St. Louis. His identification of this as a fountain is, then, not a classification but an interpretation: saying of that urinal that *it* is a fountain is indeed an instance of what I have elsewhere termed an *artistic identification*, where the "is" in question is consistent (but only consistent) with the literal falsity of the identification. Thus it is artistically true but literally false to say of a certain piece of shaped marble that it *is* St. Nicodemus, or of a certain young singer that she is the love-hungry young man Cherubino, or of a piece of fictional prose that it is a letter from Pamela. But *Campbell's Soup Can* really is a can of Campbell's soup.

Interpretations pivot on artistic identifications, and these in turn determine which parts and properties of the object in question belong to the work of art into which interpretation transfigures it. We could as easily characterize interpretations as functions which impose artworks onto material objects, in the sense of determining which properties and parts of the latter are to be taken as part of the work and as significant within the work in a way they characteristically are not outside the work. If "R. Mutt 1917" *in fact* were graffiti, it would disfigure the urinal but not necessarily the work, as a blot of spilled ink may damage a book but not in any sense affect the novel, unless the novel itself is a kind of *roman-objet* in the genre of *Tristram Shandy*. And in ruining the book it may destroy something of far greater value than the work, which may be trash. The cracks which appear in the glass panels of Duchamp's *La Mariée mise a nu par ses célébataires, même* damaged the object and obscured the work until, leaving the damaged object where it was, Duchamp made them part of the work, enlisting as unwitting collaborator the shoddy freighthandler. The object proved fragile, but it is not even remotely clear what would be meant in saying that the *work* is fragile. "Fragile" would seem not to apply to this boisterous image of oblique eroticism in which, in Richard Hamilton's words, "The Bride hangs stripped yet inviolate in her glass cage, while the bachelors grind their chocolate below." One may note, by the way, that a copy of the Great Glass would be considerably more difficult to execute than *Le Grand Verre* itself, despite which two full-scale copies of it were made, the first by Ulf Linde in 1961 and the second by Richard Hamilton, even, in 1966, at Newcastle-upon-Tyne. No one wants to take a chance shipping the original about.

I am trying to say that decisions have to be made of a sort which do not arise with mere real things. Even if one tries to cut things short by saying that the work consists in the whole damned thing, there will always remain a problem of marking the boundaries of the whole damned thing. Consider for one last time the snowshovels, and let every part of the relevant snowshovel indeed be part of *In Advance of the Broken Arm*. But what about its position? Should it be right side up or upside down, on its back or on its front? Does it or does it not make a difference? Suppose one asks, Does it mean anything that *In Advance of the Broken Arm* stands upright? The answer may be that it does not, because its having this or that position, while a property of the snowshovel, is not really a property of the work. Of an ordinary snowshovel, one again may ask what it means that it is in this position or that. But there can be no shirking at least the appropriateness of the question, for there is always, by grace of the principle of sufficient reason, an answer. (It was left just there and has not been moved. It was knocked over by the dog. It just fell.) The principle of sufficient reason also may apply to artworks, but we may be mistaken in thinking that there is something in them that requires that sort of explanation. Only what falls under an interpretation is a legitimate explanandum.

It has at times given me pleasure to imagine whole galleries of artworks from whose descriptions it could not be deduced that the material objects with which each is connected look exactly alike: galleries of snowshovels, or squares of red canvas, or paintings only one of which happens to be *The Polish Rider* of Rembrandt. The philosopher Odo Marquart has chided me for extravagance: Why not have just one square of red canvas, given the ways of the art market, and decorate the walls with interpretations? I am not sure the relationship between artwork and material object is quite so casual that the time and place and causes of the object are indifferent to the identity of the work, even though they may differ, as the date of the ready-made will differ from the date on which that particular comb has been manufactured. But this is not altogether the problem of concern to me. Rather, I am interested in the fact that the phenomenal indiscernibility of these material objects underdetermines the artworks in question in a way which must remind the sophisticates of those issues of radical translation with which W. V. Quine has plagued the philosophy of language in recent times. Even if we knew which objects were up for artistic interpretation, how could we determine which interpretation was correct? Not even Quine would wish to say that anything goes. If anything went, the skeptical problems induced by radical translation would disappear; there is the possibility of being wrong only if there is the possibility of being right. And the fact that there can be imagined countless works which look alike does not mean that countless interpretations of the same object can be given if the object is in candidacy to begin with. Modern critical theory appears to subscribe to a concept of endless interpretation, almost as though the work were after all a kind of mirror in which each of us sees something different (ourselves), and where the question of the *correct* mirror image can make no sense. I shall suppose that if there is an analogy to Quine's problem, there is meaning to the notion of being wrong, which requires that the question of correctness can arise and hence, crudely speaking, that interpretation is not endless after all.

I believe we cannot be deeply wrong if we suppose that the correct interpretation of object-as-artwork is the one which coincides most closely with the artist's own interpretation. Coinciding interpretations put us in a different posture with regard to artists than undertaking to discover what their intentions may have been; nor is it, as a thesis, subject to the sorts of objections Susan Sontag raises against interpretation generally. For the interpretations she impugns can only begin when the work of art is established as such, and the interpreter begins to ponder what the artist is "really" doing or what the work "really" means. Hers is against a notion of interpretation which makes the artwork as an explanandum—as a symptom, for example. My theory of interpretation is instead constitutive, for an object is an artwork *at all* only in relation to an interpretation. We may bring this out in a somewhat logical way. Interpretation in my sense is transfigurative. It transforms objects into works of art, and depends upon the "is" of artistic identification. Her interpretations, which are explanatory, use instead the "is" of ordinary identity. Her despised interpreters see works as signs, symptoms, expressions of ulterior or subjacent realities, states of which are what the artwork "really" refers to, and which require the interpreter to master one or another kind of code: psychoanalytical, culturographic, semiotical, or whatever. In effect, her interpreters address the work in the spirit of science, and it may very well be that the endlessness of textual interpretation derives from the endlessness of scientific perspectives under which a work may be viewed. We know too little of man, really, to pretend that no new or fresh insights into art may open up in the future. In this sense, the artist can scarcely be any more conscious of these interpretations than we are. We need not, therefore, know much about the artist when we seek to confirm these interpretations. Sontag then is arguing against *Literaturwissenschaft*, in effect: she is saying, perhaps rightly, that it will not necessarily make literature more available to us or make us better readers. She is being anti-intellectual and saying: The work gives you everything you need to know about it, if what you want is literary experience; pay attention to it. With those sorts of interpretations, the artist certainly is in no privileged position.

Mine is a theory which is in the spirit not of science but of philosophy. If interpretations are what constitute works, there are no works without them, and works are misconstituted when interpretation is wrong. Knowing the artist's interpretation is, in effect, identifying what he or she has made. The interpretation is not something outside the work: work and interpretation arise together in aesthetic consciousness. As interpretation is inseparable from work, it is inseparable from the artist if it is the artist's work.

In the case of *Fountain*, how close is my interpretation to Duchamp's? Close enough, I suppose; in any case, the work I have sought to constitute *could* be the work he made. The possible interpretations are constrained by the artist's location in the world, by when and where he lived, by what experiences he could have had. An object indiscernibly different from the one I have been discussing could have come about in many ways at many times, but the work itself could not have come about in many ways at many times and be the work it is. There is a truth to interpretation and a stability to works of art which are not relative at all.

Hayden White

The Limits
of Relativism
in the Arts

*The moment something is considered an artwork it becomes subject to
an interpretation. It owes its existence as an artwork to this, and when
its claim to art is defeated, it loses its interpretation and becomes a
mere thing.*

Arthur C. Danto

*The specific function of modern didactic art has been to show that art
does not reside in material entities, but in relations between people and
between people and the components of their environment.*

Jack Burnham

*In this end of the twentieth century we now know that art does indeed
exist as an idea. And we know that quality exists in the thinking of the
artist, not in the object he employs—if he employs any object at all.*

Donald Karshan

On the most abstract level, the question of relativism is inti-
mately bound up with the problem of essences.[1] If objects have
essential natures, then neither their meaning nor their value is
relative; meaning and value would not inhere in the relationships that objects sustain with other objects, and neither their
meaning nor their value would change as these relationships
changed. If, on the other hand, objects do not have essential
natures, their only possible meaning or value would be that
which inheres in their relationships with other objects. If these

relationships were to change, the meaning and value of these objects would also change. And this, I take it, is the essence of the relativist position.

Now, this position does not necessarily imply that we cannot have knowledge of a non-relativistic sort about objects, their relationships with other objects, or the changes that these might undergo. One can be a relativist with respect to the question of the meaning or value of specific objects, and a non-relativist with respect to the kind of knowledge that one can have about the kinds of meaning and value that objects possess in their different relationships with other objects. The question of the truth of propositions about the meaning or value of objects can be detached from the question of the meaning and value that objects possess in different relationships.

Of course, in order to detach the two questions, one must believe that there is at least one object—namely, the knowing subject—which bears a special kind of relationship to any object coming under its scrutiny. Or one must believe that there is at least one kind of object—namely, propositions or predications—that bears the special relationship of truthfulness to other kinds of objects. On this view, objects are not conceived to *be* true or false. They may or may not possess meaning or value, but this has nothing to do with their truthfulness. One can argue that this is true even of the kind of object which is the knowing subject. As object, the knowing subject may not possess truthfulness; it may possess meaning or value, just like any other object, depending on the relationship that it sustains with other objects in its various contexts; but as object it possesses neither truthfulness nor falsity. Propositions alone are true or false, and one can be a relativist about meaning and value while remaining a non-relativist about the question of the truthfulness and falsity of propositions. Only if one conceived of the truthfulness or falsity of all propositions as inhering in changeable relationships with their referents could one be considered an *absolute* relativist.

By now, philosophers will be growing restless, if not irritated, about these crude formulations of the "problem" of relativism. But crude or not, the formulation is, I trust, a fair representation of one of the enduring commonplaces of critics' discussions of this problem. For as everyone knows, one can hold the *absolute* relativist position only in paradox. The proposition that the truth or falsity of all propositions inheres in their relationships with their referents, that these relationships may change and therewith that their truth or falsity may change also—this is itself an absolute, not a relative, proposition. And it is open to the objections conventionally advanced against the "liar's paradox."

Yet, the weight of the liar's paradox critique depends upon the *belief* that paradoxical statements or sets of statements cannot be truthful. If one believes that relationships in reality itself are contradictory, then paradoxical propositions would not be subject to criticism based on the liar's paradox argument. This conviction seems to lie behind Derrida's disquieting attacks on referentiality, perception, and valorization in any form.[2] And these attacks have at least forced us to reflect on the fact that, in matters of belief or conviction, paradox is no sin. Indeed, it is not even a mistake, as the history of religion amply shows.

Why should statements or chains of statements *not* be paradoxical? Is it not possible that John is both good and evil, both beautiful and ugly, attractive and repulsive, wise and stupid, learned and ignorant, at one and the same time? If one holds that the only truth that matters is that which recognizes the contradictory nature of reality (or of the relationship between human consciousness and its possible objects of cognition), is one a relativist or a non-relativist? This was Hegel's question—a question discussed at length in his *Logic*—and he certainly did not believe himself to be a relativist even despite his conviction that all of the knowledge we possess was, in a crucial sense, paradoxical.[3] For him, a logic based on the principles of identity and non-contradiction could not serve as a universally valid criterion for assessing the truthfulness of statements about reality. On the contrary, for him the principle of non-contradiction had only a relative value; it obtained only for those statements having to do with objects permanently fixed in their natures (for him, dead matter on the one hand, and God on the other). Everything in between, everything capable of undergoing development (or actualization)—which in itself bespoke a certain inadequacy between what it was and what it might still yet become—could be viewed as a kind of living contradiction and appropriately spoken about only in the mode of paradox or antinomy.

It is a commonplace of modern aesthetics that artworks can be regarded as true or false only insofar as they predicate. Do artworks, even literary artworks, poems and novels, for example, predicate? Obviously they contain predications ("This is the way the world ends"; "A rose is a rose") and they may even "add up" to a single large predication ("Life is a battlefield"; "War is hell"). Does this mean that we would be acting appropriately to rush out and subject them to tests of verification or falsification? Or not even to "rush out," but simply to "wait and see"? Obviously not; as everyone recognizes, to do so would be to display the kind of foolishness about which Cervantes wrote a long novel. Even those who think that novels or poems possess a *kind* of truth would think it tactless to regard whatever truth they do possess as subject to empirical verification or falsification. Meaning (or meanings), surely; value (or values), certainly; but empirically verifiable (or falsifiable) truthfulness, *no*.

Of course, a work of art may conform to some conception of "the way things really are" which I or the group to which I belong and from which I gain my sense of public identity may hold as an article of faith. But when I or the group to which I belong cease to exist, even this correspondence is dissolved, and the work of art is left without a referent (i.e., our "conception"). So, with respect to the possible truthfulness that a work of art may possess, even insofar as it predicates, this is a relative matter at best. Only if I believe in certain absolute and changeless truths, which must appear like propositions written by the hand of God in some imagined heavenly book, can I believe that a work of art which predicates might possess truthfulness. And it would be "truthful" only insofar as its predications matched up with those written by God or inscribed in a consciousness inhabiting some place beyond time and space.

Well, if not truthfulness, what about meaning and value? I assume that works of art might contain not one iota of truth and still possess meaning. A representation of the sun god in an ancient Egyptian stela would be meaningful without being in the least truthful. What kind of meaning would it possess? A meaning that is purely contingent, based upon its correspondence to what people of a certain time, place, and cultural endowment believed to be the appropriate way to produce meaningful representations. To be sure, we often come upon artifacts which, although they seem to be meaningless, still seem to be identifiable as works of art; but such artifacts can qualify as works of art only insofar as we can impute to them a "meaning" construed as the "function" they must have had in the culture that produced them. Here we are verging once more on a relativistic notion of meaning, for any given artifact has more than one function, can be *used* for different purposes, can have a use function or an exchange function, and its meaning can therefore be construed as variable, relative to the use to which it is put at a given time and place.

What are we to do with those artifacts which, although they

appear to be artistic in nature, come unattended by any testimony concerning their original function? Many Etruscan artifacts had functions which we either do not know or can only surmise. If the meaning is the function, then we must take a relativistic perspective on the question of meaning. Some other kind of meaning must be conceived if we are to escape relativism.

One alternative might be to construe the meaning of an artifact in terms of the cultural code of which it is an instantiation. This would give us a notion of meaning that would be intrinsic, non-referential, epideictic. We could say that the meaning of the artifact is given less in the use that is made of it than in what it instantiates, and that what it instantiates is the code or codes available at the time of its creation for the production of meaning. Here "meaningfulness" would be a product of nothing more than the proper application of the rules for producing meaningful things obtaining in a given time and place. But then meaningfulness becomes identified with rule-governed creativity; if and when the rules are changed, the meaning of any artifact constructed on the basis of prior rules must be changed, too. So here, too, we are driven toward a relativist position. Michelangelo is reputed to have answered a critic of one of his portraits, who complained about its lack of verisimilitude to its subject, with the rejoinder: Who will know the difference a hundred years from now? Was he suggesting that the meaning of the portrait, not to speak of its truthfulness, resided in the perfection of his enactment of the code of portrait painting, which he took to be eternal? Or was he suggesting that a portrait might have many meanings, the dominant one of which changed with every change in the constituency of its viewers? Or was he suggesting that the meaning or truthfulness of the portrait mattered less than its *value* as a work of art produced by him, the master?

Value. Surely this is the nub of the matter, what is really at issue in the question of "relativism in the arts." For it is the value of art as one activity among many in culture and the value of one or more artworks among all of the artifacts claiming title to being artworks that ultimately interests critics and theorists, and even practicing artists. Truthfulness we can give up, along with referentiality; meaning we can problematize, along with the very notion of culture. Both of these notions are tied to culture-specific conceptions of art that we have abandoned or at least radically questioned. But value is another matter. If artistic activity does not possess a value different from and superior to other kinds of cultural activity, and if some artworks do not possess a value superior to that of others, then what is aesthetics to deal with, much less the art market trade in?

Arthur Danto suggests that the value of a work of art is as changeable as the various historical contexts in which it may be assigned to or withdrawn from the category of the artistic.[4] Notice that he does not question the reality of or the value of art, either as an activity or as a category to which works may be variably assigned. On the contrary, he believes that art is as valuable as the activity of interpretation which he takes to be the occasion for recognizing that an artifact has been moved into the category of the artistic. He does suggest that it is the decision or impulse to interpret that constitutes a given artifact as an artwork, rather than the other way around. For him, artifacts do not always require (claim) interpretation; it is when they become subjects for interpretation that they are constituted as artworks. Therefore the status as well as the value of an artifact as an artwork is constituted by someone's impulse to treat it as an object to be interpreted. Its being so treated is a function of the art-historical context in which it finds itself. This is, if I may borrow a term from Marx,[5] a use-notion of value: the value of the artwork is relative to the use to which it is put as an object of interpretation by someone at some particular place and time.

This view has the merit (or shortcoming, depending on how one views the matter) of at least dissociating the value of artworks from their function in an exchange system. No one would be willing to argue that the value of an artwork is to be equated with that of other objects or commodities for which it might be exchanged. That would be a vulgar kind of relativism indeed. It would make the artwork a commodity exactly like any other commodity insofar as its value could be indicated by the kind of commodity for which it could be exchanged, and it would be relativistic insofar as the market in which the artwork circulated would be as variable as that reported in the daily tallies of the New York Stock Exchange, with some items soaring to the tops of the preferred lists one day and plummeting the next, in accordance with the laws of supply and demand.

At best, the notion of the artwork as a commodity precisely like other commodities would allow us to envision only the *social* function of art and artworks, which is precisely equivalent to its exchange function. The *use* to which any commodity, including the art commodity, may be put varies from individual to individual. We can imagine the fetishist who might find in a given work of art a peculiar fascination which would endow it with a value, in his eyes, quite incommensurable with its value in the eyes of any other person. Exchange value is quite different from use value, more "objective" we might say, since it is established by the capacity of the commodity in exchange to *command* a valorization sufficient to induce the one who desires it to surrender something of worth in his own eyes in order to gain possession of it.

But if exchange value is more objective than use value, it is nonetheless just as relative, rising and falling according to laws of supply and demand, fashion, taste, and the like—all notoriously unstable phenomena, even if we are able to plot curves of their variations in statistical distributions.

What other kind of value could we invoke in order to characterize the nature of the artwork, that which at once links it to other commodities insofar as it shares with them both an exchange and use value, but differs from them *qualitatively* so as to liberate it from the relativism to which these latter indenture it? There is, of course, labor value, which has the indubitable virtue of being agreed upon as the absolute criterion of worth by classical political economists like Locke and Smith on the one side and Marxists on the other. But do we wish to say that the *value* of the artwork, like that of other commodities, actually consists of the "amount of socially necessary labor power expended in its production"? The idea is attractive if only because it removes the notion of real value from the threat of relativism.

The real value of any commodity, according to Marx, consists of the human labor power "congealed" within it as an essence *different in kind* from that which is expended by other animals, such as bees and beavers, in the production of their artifacts. While the amount of "socially necessary labor power" expended in the production of any given commodity may change with changes in the modes of production prevailing in a given society (so that, for example, the amount expended in the production of a pair of shoes in fourteenth-century Paris differs from that so expended in nineteenth-century London), the value of the products of the two processes remains relatable to the quotients of human labor-power invested in each. And mind you, Marx *does* distinguish among different kinds of labor, mental and physical, artistic and artisanal, hand and machine, and so forth; he leaves no doubt that mental or imaginative labor creates a commodity different in kind from that produced by animal instinct and a resultant physical activity alone.[6] Once a *qualitative* distinction has been permitted to creep into the discussion of commodity value, it is difficult to see how it can be denied admission to any effort to discriminate among different kinds of humanly produced commodities. So, here at least, on grounds that are neither specifically Marxist nor specifically bourgeois, but are shared by both camps in what is otherwise a veritable Manichaean division over most questions, we have a way of evading a drift into relativism. Only if we believed that human labor does *not* differ essentially, in quality, from animal labor would we be inclined to reduce all products of all labor processes to the same kind and to say that our impulse to call certain commodities artistic is a purely relative matter, dependent upon the various *uses* to which individuals might put them or their *functions* in the various exchange systems in which they might circulate.

Commodities differ from one another in at least three ways, then: in the *uses* to which they can be put, in their *functions* in exchange systems, and in the *kinds of labor* expended in their production. The first two categories give us good reasons for thinking about commodities in a relativistic way; the third permits us to imagine qualitative distinctions among them. But the qualitative distinctions alluded to have to do with those between products of animal labor, on the one hand, and products of human labor, on the other. If we are to follow Marx a bit further, we must distinguish between those commodities that are products predominantly of imaginative labor and those that are products of more mechanical operations. In saying "imaginative labor" one does not have to be understood to be invoking some "spiritual" agency; we need only attempt to specify the attribute of the humanly produced artifact that makes it distinguishable from its animally produced counterpart. And whatever other differences there may be between them, it seems undeniable that one feature of humanly produced artifacts marks them as different: this is their *symbolizing* function. The difficulty here is how to talk about symbols, or symbolization, without falling into mysticism.

This danger can perhaps be avoided by calling upon some modern theories of signification which distinguish among signs that are indexical, signs that are iconic, and signs that are symbolic.[7] Indexical and iconic signs are found in nature; their presence need not be taken as indicating any conscious intentionality or purpose informing their production. But symbolizing signs require that we impute intention or purpose to them, if not to the consciousness of their producers. Following Nelson Goodman (on whose work much of what follows depends),[8] we may say that signs symbolize insofar as their status as examples, representations, or expressions can be comprehended only by way of an understanding of the codes they employ in the process of their production. These codes may vary from culture to culture and from epoch to epoch in a given culture's evolution, and in such a way as to determine the limits of what can be symbolized in a given sign system. What a given symbolic system *can* signify must be seen as relative to the code or codes of signification of which it is an application. But this has to do with the *meaning or truthfulness* of a given symbolizing artifact, not with its *value as an index* of a crucial difference between uniquely human processes of signification and their counterparts in the animal world. This marks an absolute difference between the two kinds of processes.

So, too, with respect to the value that we might wish to assign to different instantiations of the symbol-producing capacity of human beings. Here we can invoke the principle that more valuable artifacts display the effects of the widest, fullest, or most subtle powers of the human capacity to produce symbols and symbol systems. This line of thought might even yield another criterion for discriminating among different products of that ca-

pacity; that is, the evidence in them of the relative degree of
self-consciousness displayed in the production of a given symbol
system. This would be consistent, I would hope, with Jakobson's
famous insistence that the literary (or poetic) work differs from
the non-literary work by virtue of its apparent self-referentiality,[9]
its way of calling attention to or featuring as part of its "content"
its own symbolizing process. This is also what is intended, I
surmise, by the formalist notion that "form" is among the various "contents" that one can specify in any work of literary art.
The form of the work is one of its own contents. The medium
may not be the whole message, but it is certainly a part of the
message, since any message of a peculiarly human sort is always
also—in addition to whatever information, command, or predication it may contain—*about* (makes reference to, draws attention to) its own medium of transmission. This is not to say that
artworks do not always have extrinsic referents; on the contrary,
it is to say that they are intra- as well as extra-referential, that
they refer to themselves as well as to whatever it is beyond themselves that they exemplify, represent, or express.

As you can see, this gives some grounds for speaking about
the power of a given human artifact to *claim* interpretation. But
here the impulse to interpret is not considered to arise from a
purely subjective or contextually determined *decision* on the
part of someone to *treat* a given object as *requiring* interpretation. There are objects which demand interpretation because
they contain such a "repleteness," such a "density" of symbolizing content that they resist consignment to the category of the
immediately comprehensible.[10] The decision to treat an object
as requiring interpretation comes about when an artist or critic
decides to treat *as if* it were a *symbol* some sign which is manifestly a product of natural or mechanical processes. In this regard, Duchamp's famous gesture in bringing the urinal into an
art exhibit and displaying it in a context which suggested that

it should be treated in the same way that one might have previously treated the *Mona Lisa* can be seen as a creative gesture precisely insofar as it is a *symbolizing* gesture. The urinal itself is properly subject to "interpretation" only as a cultural *index* or, insofar as it might resemble some other artifact, as an *icon*. A symbolic dimension might be said to have been created by the *presence* of the urinal in a cultural context in which such objects had not been previously displayed; but in this case the interpretative impulse is not a specifically aesthetic one. Here the interpretative impulse arises from the sensed incongruity of two cultural codes brought into juxtaposition, the code of excrementary disposal and that of aesthetic expectations. The urinal itself is not a proper subject of a specifically aesthetic interpretation except insofar as it might possess the kind of symbolic density and repleteness that objects fashioned with a higher degree of imaginative self-consciousness can be said to possess. (One can conceive of an *art nouveau* urinal, for example.)

We value works of art and artifacts *as* works of art for different reasons, to be sure, but we value them above all for the consciousness that they induce in us of our generally shared human powers of symbolizing. Any cultural artifact may induce such self-consciousness, to be equally sure, but our interest in some artifact that comes to us from a remote culture the symbolic dimensions of which we find difficult to specify is surely different from our interest in artifacts utilizing relatively familiar codes of symbolization whose richness, fullness, and subtlety we can appreciate even when we cannot duplicate them. This is why what may be considered a work of art in a culture different from our own may not be so considered by us. Such artifacts may very well invite, engage, or otherwise "claim" our interpretative interest, but insofar as they remain effectively *uninterpretable* (remain opaque, do not yield to our need to identify the multiplicity of symbolizing processes involved in their production), they remain equally difficult to bring into the sphere of the artistic, at least insofar as this sphere can be envisaged only from the standpoint of the value we attach to the symbolizing process.

You will readily recognize that this conception of the artwork shares much with the ideas of critics like Harold Bloom, who holds that we value poetry insofar as it provides us with a kind of model of the constitutive process which occurs in the production of a self.[11] But Bloom inclines to exclude from the category of significant artworks those poems that do not symbolize this process of self-production in specifically Oedipal terms. Nonetheless, I share with him the notion that the process of self-production is a process of self-symbolization, a symbolization of the self to the self, and that this process is the ground of and the reason for our interest in those cultural artifacts which, *because they symbolize this process of self-symbolization*, seem to *demand* our interpretative interest and which, as a result, we apprehend as being artworks.

Considerations such as these surely lie behind the impulse, growing stronger everywhere, to collapse the distinction between the critical and the creative performance,[12] as when we are inclined to view the kind of virtuoso critical talents displayed by Barthes or Derrida in their writings as being no less "artistic" or "creative" for being at the same time "critical" and "derivative." Such considerations also, I surmise, lie behind the current celebration of *reading* as an artistic activity every bit as "creative" as the activity of writing that provides this reading with its occasions, which theorists such as Fish, Holland, and Barthes himself have recently set forth.[13] Reading or, as its equivalent in the visual and plastic arts is called, "beholding," is a process of symbol production and integration every bit as instructive of the processes by which our selves are constituted as anything found on a printed page or canvas. This is true even though the product may appear not in the form of a material entity but only as a heightened sense in the reader or beholder of the ideal of symbol production to which the ideal of self-production bears some kind of relationship: of resemblance, analogy, homology, or affinity. Whether the self envisioned as the product of this process is conceived as an individual or as a collective phenomenon, the process of its production through symbolization is a constant throughout. This may be why it is possible for us to appreciate as art, even when we do not understand what is being said or represented in it, some artifact that comes to us from a culture so "exotic" that we comprehend nothing of the specific codes utilized in its original creation.

Consider, by way of example of some of the problems arising from this formulation, the kind of cave paintings, dating from the Paleolithic period, found at Lascaux.[14] Surely there is something anachronistic in our wishing to consider them *as art*, since it is difficult to imagine that, given the stage in the evolution of their culture, the peoples of that time could have conceived of the category of the "artistic" as a distinctive kind of activity. I find it difficult to imagine that the earliest viewers of these works (if there were viewers) could have been conscious of the activity of "interpretation" which we conceive ourselves to engage in when we try to make sense of them—speculating about their function in the culture that produced them, imagining how they might have been apprehended by their original viewers, and so on. A cultural behaviorist, of course, would not raise questions of this sort, since from this point of view such "paintings" could have only an iconic or indexical function, rather than a symbolizing one. Some of the paintings are undeniably representational, and we can even identify their referents—what they seem to have been intended to represent. Insofar as the identification of their representational contents might successfully close off inquiry, it might even be said, following Danto, that they have ceased to have a "claim" on our interpretative impulses as specifically artistic works.

But can they be said to *exemplify* or to *express*? This is a different question, requiring different mental operations for their elaboration. A work of art can be construed to be an exemplification of something in the mode of symbolization without being so intended by its creator. What would it be an example of? Well, obviously, of the symbolizing process itself. And what is the nature of this exemplification? It is that of a species of one or another of the genera of symbolizing activities which we must assume to be common to human beings wherever they have appeared. I say "a species" rather than "an individual" exemplification, since the cave painters display species attributes more manifestly than they display an identifiable person's creative talents. The more a given work displays the creative power of an identifiable person, the more the "style" of symbolization approximates what Richard Wollheim calls a "signature"; the more it falls into the category of expressiveness, rather than that of exemplification.[15] But it is the process of symbolization by which, say, an emotion is expressed or a class of things is exemplified that leads us to value a given artifact as an artwork, rather than any attachment we may have to *what* is expressed or exemplified in a specific work.

In certain hieratic traditions of symbolization the exemplifying moment predominates, as Gombrich has argued in *Art and Illusion*;[16] and the representational moment (at least as that moment is understood in Western realistic artistic practices) is weakened, and the expressive moment is all but totally suppressed. The so-called realism of Western art, by contrast, features the combination of exemplification and representation—or, rather, representation by exemplification—in its dominant strain, with the expressive moment coming to the fore as the conventions of this kind of realism are progressively worked through in the nineteenth century. But the appeal, the constant interest we have in the achievement of the great nineteenth-century realists (from David to Cézanne, from Diderot to Zola) has less to do with their success in truly representing the world given to perception than in the subtlety with which they worked through the problem of *symbolizing by means of representation*,[17] as against the means of expression, on the one side, or those of exemplification, on the other. These works demand interpretation, "claim" it, while continually resisting *definitive* interpretation, precisely because they symbolically represent the process of representation itself. That is to say, they both *enact* and *draw attention to* at the same time. Insofar as the process of representation is a generally cultural and therefore generally human activity, it is difficult to imagine that these works could ever be demoted to the category of the non-artistic, whatever lack of interest a given generation of viewers might have in them. Because they are representations of representation—symbols of the process of representation, rather than merely reports about perceptions made in the medium of paint on canvas—they can never *finally* be fully interpretable.

In this the works of the realist period differ from those reports about the world set forth in the form of predications or constative utterances which do not emit signals indicative of the problematicity of their own enactment—as a certain kind of artifact, which may conveniently be called "journalistic," always seeks to do. I say "seeks to do" because even the plainest discourse or image, just by virtue of being a symbolization, bears the marks of the condition of its own production, calls attention to its efforts to symbolize effectively, if only by the systematic suppression of conventional stylistic or signatory markers. What makes such utterances not very interesting as objects of interpretation is that they do not manifestly (i.e., by the form in which they come clothed) suggest that they have been created in any self-conscious awareness of the problem of symbolization. People who do not know that they are speaking prose are inclined to produce the kind of prose that is both very full and very empty of symbolic content. It is very full because such a speaker is at the mercy of the symbolic code, usually some kind of common sense, that he unthinkingly uses as the only possible way of truthfully representing reality. It is very empty because it does not display any consciousness of the fact that things can be represented just as effectively, given different purposes and contexts, in some other code or codes.

Commonsensical thought and its usual carrier, plain speech, are, like prehistoric art, devoid of any indications of an awareness of the possibility of a choice among alternative ways of symbolizing. They are weak in material for interpretation because they do not display any awareness that the creation, transmission, and reception of messages all involve choices among alternative modes of symbolization. In this respect they do not differ from stones, trees, or natural objects. They may possess the kind of *contingent* signification that a stone, fashioned by climatic wear and tear into a semblance of another object, such as an egg or an arrowhead, can have; or the kind of *necessary* signification that moss may possess by virtue of its location on the side of a tree that remains unexposed to direct sunlight. They might well be the occasion of an interpretative inquiry that would center upon their iconic or indexical status. But such journalistic artifacts can be said to lack evidence of a high degree of symbolic content precisely in the extent to which they yield to our understanding of them *as* icons or indices. The artful suppression of the constructed nature of one's own discourse may itself be a highly symbolic gesture, but the product of that suppression is unlikely to be very rich in symbolic content. Its manifest denial of any need to be interpreted, its insistence that it be taken "at face value" as a discourse that has resisted the impulse to represent its contents symbolically, would place it in the category of the artistic only insofar as this refusal implicitly suggested reference to the problematicity of interpretation itself. But any discourse that simply ignored the problem of either symbolization or interpretation on its manifest level can be rightfully denied membership in the category of artifacts that we call "artistic."

To insist that symbolization is a necessary condition of artworks is not to say that all symbolizing artifacts are artistic; nor is it to pretend to address the question of the ultimate nature of symbolization, the possible modes of symbolization, or the social function of symbolizing processes. It seems difficult not to see symbolization as the necessary precondition of those processes of exchange which we designate as specifically cultural, in contrast to those called natural. We might wish to say that symbolization, like the prohibition on incest as Lévi-Strauss conceived it, belongs neither to nature nor to culture but is the very point or threshold at which nature becomes transformed into culture.[18] Insofar as a natural object is transformed into an object capable of taking its place in the circulation of commodities in culture, it is so transformed by some expenditure of human labor, a labor which endows it with a meaning (what we might call a use meaning or an exchange meaning) that is symbolic in nature. Surely the specific use to which the fetishist might wish to put any given object has to do with the value he assigns that object in a mode of signification that can only be called symbolic. So, too, the capacity of any given object to function as an exchange item in a specific system of commodity circulation has to do with its being endowed with a value that is equally symbolic, though in this case public rather than private—symbolic of the value of the object for which it might be exchanged. The "true" value of any commodity may be, as Marx says, the amount of socially necessary labor expended in its production; but the manifestation of this quotient of labor, however we might wish to calculate it, is contained in its capacity to function as a symbol. That symbol may represent a certain set of use values; or it may represent a certain notion of value itself, the notion which makes it possible to imagine that one commodity may have value equivalent to another in a given system of exchange.

We might wish to distinguish between the system of *social* exchange which prevails in a given time and place, and which centers on commodities as such, and the system of *cultural* exchange which centers upon the perceived relative worth of commodities in their function as carriers of symbolic contents. This would allow us to account for the differences between the apparent relativity of the value of artworks in their social dimension as against the absolute value they possess in their cultural dimension. As thus viewed, the insistence that the value of artworks is purely relative to the value that they are accorded by different groups or individuals at different times and places would not be false but only half-true, i.e., true in the extent to which what was being indicated here was their function in systems of commodity exchange for use. In such systems the symbolic content of any artifact will be valued or devalued (even to the point at which the artifact is denied membership in the category of artworks) solely in response to the exigencies of the art market, changes in public or private taste, preferences of collectors, and the like. When used as a basis for arguing the relativism of the value of *all* works of art, as in certain sociologies of art, it can be easily seen that this argument amounts to little more than a generalization from the social to the cultural dimensions of the artwork's existence. This brand of relativism fails to take into account the extent to which artworks are *transportable* across the boundaries marking the difference between one social system and another. In other words, it fails to distinguish between social exchange and cultural exchange. In the latter the symbolic content of the artifact makes it transculturally circulatable, in the way that an item that is primarily produced for a certain practical use is not.

An exchange of symbols has no function other than a cultural one. When symbols, rather than utilitarian items, are being exchanged, we have a specifically cultural rather than a specifically social act. The *sociality* of the act of cultural exchange may be contained in the items for use of which the exchange of symbols is itself symbolic,[19] but the *culturality* of the act is contained in the symbols that attend the exchange of items for use. It is the symbols that require interpretation, not the items for use which they symbolize. Where symbols are exchanged, merely social relationships are transformed into cultural relationships. The presence of symbols makes human social exchanges qualitatively different from their animal simulacra—*pace* the sociobiologists, who appear incapable of differentiating the exchanges of signs that are iconic or indexical from those that are symbolic.

Where symbolization is present, art is also present—perhaps not recognized as such, but present nonetheless. Insofar as any artifact is capable of being exchanged because of its symbolic (rather than its utilitarian) nature, we may be sure that the kind of activity we recognize as artistic has been expended in its production. This is no doubt why it is rather easy to displace attitudes and feelings that religious cultures lavish on their sacred objects onto the kinds of objects that we call artistic. We resist radical relativism in the arts because we wish to believe that art is a product of a human capacity that was once attributed only to God. This limit on the impulse to relativize art and artworks may be the result of a residual religiosity or idealism in our secularist thinking, but it is also an intuition of the kind of value

that human beings are able to produce by the kind of symbolizing labor that we can *see* went into the production of certain
kinds of commodities as against others.

The insistence on the differences between artistic and other
kinds of human activity is not a result (or not *only* a result) of
that socially determined attitude toward culture that we label
"aestheticist." It manifests a universal recognition that the basis
of human culture itself, whatever local differences may separate
any given incarnation of it from any other, resides in the human
capacity to symbolize.

Having raised the question of the relationship between art and
religion, a word should be said about the artistic status of artifacts manifestly produced for extra-artistic but nonetheless
higher cultural purposes: Gothic cathedrals, ritual vessels, sacer-
dotal robes, and the like. In my view, we detract not at all from
the artistic status of such works by granting that they were prin-
cipally intended to serve another, generally utilitarian and specifically religious purpose. Indeed, the artistic nature of such
artifacts is all the more evident in the extent to which they bear
indications of the symbolic functions that they were intended to
fulfill *in addition to* their primary purpose (to serve as a place of
worship; to hold the sacramental wine or host; to clothe the
priest). In one description of such artifacts we may be inclined
to demote them from the category of the artistic to that of the artisanal; this is a relative matter, having to do with prevailing opin-
ions concerning the extent to which genuinely artistic works
must rise above the restraints placed upon their creation by ritual or other utilitarian considerations. It might be better to say
that such works, while being artistic insofar as they bear evidence
of their maker's awareness of the problems of symbolization, are
products of artistic conventions that feature exemplification and
representation over expression in their production. Surely there
is nothing wrong with saying that a work can have a utilitarian

function and an artistic form at one and the same time. It does not cease being an artistic work, any more than it ceases being a commodity, simply by virtue of its being put to one use rather than to some other. But it is not made *more* artistic by being removed from its ritual or generally utilitarian function and being placed in an art gallery for viewing or for sale. The extent of its value as an artistic work is marked by the range of response that it induces as an object, not of interpretation, but of self-consciousness about the symbolizing process of which it is an instantiation, in its beholders.

The same kind of question arises when we try to think through the relationship between genres of discourse. A philosophical discourse is not rendered less philosophical by being proven faulty in its reasoning and assigned to the category of works expressive of a point of view once held to be valid but no longer considered so.[20] Nor is a philosophical discourse appropriately conceived to be an artwork only when, although generally considered to be wrong or wrongheaded, it is still read and appreciated for its "style" (usually a synonym for wit, liveliness, etc.). If such a discourse is conceived to possess these attributes at some point in the history of its reception by different groups of readers, it must have possessed them all along, even while it still passed for "straightforward" or "serious" philosophical discourse, rather than for "literature" or a "document" in the history of ideas. All that the impulse to change a discourse from the category of philosophy to that of literature indicates is that it has passed out of the system of social circulation and into that of cultural circulation. This is a relative matter, depending on what can count as "philosophical" and what as (merely) "literary" at different times and places in any given society's history. But the capacity of a discourse to function in the cultural system is evidence of the power that enabled it to function in the social system originally. Indeed, if a philosophical discourse comes to be adjudged wrong or no longer admissable to what counts as philosophy, its original attraction for those who once counted as "philosophers" can only be accounted for by the valorization that it must earlier have been accorded on its artistic merits, i.e., its powers of effective symbolization.

The problem of the artifact created for a specifically non-artistic function (such as ritual) or as a place to house non-artistic activities (such as worship) is much like that which arises with respect to the philosophical discourse that is sometimes during its career appreciated *only* for its literary (i.e., artistic) features. What we should say about artifacts translated from one category (say, the religious) to another (say, the artistic) is not that they suddenly *become* "artistic" by virtue of this translation, but that their symbolic function is now valued for different reasons. Their symbolizing power will not have changed, since the artifact is the same as it was before the translation; rather, we now release this power from its service to specifically religious uses and fix our attention upon it as an end in itself. To be sure, a radical relativist might say that what we mean by symbolization or the capacity or evidence of the capacity to symbolize is a relative matter, dependent upon what we understand a "symbol" to be, do, or consist of. That might be true, but so far as I can see it would in no way endanger the thesis that we value works of art for their symbolizing power, whatever our notion of the *nature* of symbolization itself.

This mélange of Marxist, semiological, para-philosophical, and historical reflections that I have presented contains nothing that is not derivative, and it may well constitute less a consideration of the nature of artworks than a defense of symbolization in the interest of *setting* limits (rather than *finding* them) on a relativism to which, on epistemic grounds, I am generally most sympathetic. This limit-setting seems necessary not because relativistic ideas are rampant amongst artists and art critics, but because, in the movements known as structuralism and post-structuralism, the attack upon the very notion of value has been launched on grounds that can be legitimately interpreted as constituted by an attack upon the very notion of symbolization. For both structuralists and post-structuralists, the basic unit of meaning-value is not the symbol but the sign, the distinguishing aspect of which is the arbitrariness of its conjunctions of signifiers (sounds or images) with signifieds (the concepts which these evoke). The symbol is thus reduced to the status of being *nothing but* a system of signification that has become conventionalized in a given culture or social group. Not only is there no such thing as a "natural symbol" (the title of a well-known book by Mary Douglas, who is a kind of structuralist anthropologist), neither is there any such thing as a system of cultural symbols adequate to represent the world it seeks to exemplify, describe, or express in signs. The human capacity to create symbol systems is thus envisaged as little more than a basis for understanding how human intelligence can bewitch itself by its own powers of signification. These powers of self-bewitchment are so considerable as to separate permanently consciousness from its objects or referents. The whole process of signification is reduced to the status of an endless chain of displacements and inversions of signifiers that constantly turn back upon themselves and turn themselves inside out, like a Moebius strip (a favorite simile in these movements), but without ever getting closer to the world it wishes to signify.

The heuristic power of this formulation is indeed formidable, and only a kind of professional parochialism would deny the benefits that have accrued from the execution of the structuralist/post-structuralist enterprise. But the view of signification which informs this enterprise can lead to the obscuring of two factors bearing on the questions of the meaning, truth, and value of any instance of signification. One factor is contained in the fact that the self-referential argument cuts two ways: if language or poetic or artistic signs in general are always in some way self-referential, it follows that such signs possess their own referents within themselves and, unlike animal or natural signs, feature themselves as elements in their own elaboration or articulation. This means that the truth or meaning they contain is more analytic than synthetic, but it is a *kind* of truth or meaning nonetheless. The other factor has to do with the value of signification. Self-referentiality may be taken as an advantage that human signification enjoys over animal signification, and this advantage may arise precisely in the service that symbolization can render to the project of self-referentiality. It does not follow that, because the union of the signifier and the signified is arbitrary, the product of that union is valueless or only relatively valuable. The worth of the arbitrariness of that union is that it points to the capacity of human beings to create or endow things with a meaning they do not naturally possess, a meaning which they possess only by virtue of the fact that they have been turned into symbols. The *meanings* of these artifacts may be relative to the *uses* made of them in a given culture, but the *value* of such artifacts resides in the extent to which they remind us that meaning itself is created by human beings, rather than found in nature. Since art is the activity par excellence in which this process of self-symbolization is worked through, examined, investigated, experimented with, revised, elaborated, and articulated, it does not seem too much to grant the relativists their contention that the *meaning* of any artifact, and perhaps even its *truth*, can be contingent in some way, while keeping faith with the intuition that art's *value* lies precisely in its power to remind us of how much of the meaning we find in the world is a product of the power of human beings to turn error into truth, misunderstanding into comprehension, and even poetry into science—by means of symbolization.

But what about Derrida, who must be on everyone's mind? What about his brand of relativism, if such it be? I am inclined to think that he is not a relativist at all, or that he is one only in an instrumentalist way, in preparation for the kind of mysticism represented by the poet Edmund Jabès.[21] Derrida's principal enemy is certain fetishisms of Western thought: the origin, the subject, referentiality, closure. He seems to leave nothing undeconstructed, to leave nothing possessed of the originary self-certitude or even the organized anxiety that must have inspired its creation in the first place. Paul de Man is even more radical—he not only deconstructs discourse but also claims to be able to show how discourses, whether in prose or in poetry, whether lyric, epic, or dramatic, and presumably whether written in ink, etched in stone, or set forth in lines and colors, *deconstruct themselves*, anticipate their own failures, seek to guard against them, and *in the best cases* turn their own anticipated failures into their own subject matter. This seems to be an attack not only on the possibility of unambiguous meaning and unassailable truth, but on value itself. For is not a discourse which fails, even if it tries to take account of its own imminent failure and somehow to convert this failure into a kind of success, is not such discourse diminished in value by being diminished in meaning or truth?

I do not think so. It depends on whether you vest the value of an object in its status as a product or in the process by which it was produced. In showing the instability of the product, the discourse, or the representation, Derrida and de Man implicitly valorize the process of production. Their critical exercises always show how a product worthy of interpretation bears the marks of the process of its own production on its very surface, in such a way that this productive process, this poiesis, becomes the object of their analytical or interpretative enterprises.[22] To defetishize the object is to show how it bears the marks of a purely human process; this is the consistent effect, if not the explicit aim, of their critical labor. To show how artworks may fail to achieve perfect closure, absolute truth, and ultimate meaning is not to show that they are worthless. It is only to show that they are products of *human* creativity, rather than of senseless laws of nature or of an imagined divine author of the world.

The famous aporia which critics like de Man, Miller, Hartman, and others find at the absent center of every text may very well indicate the fatal flaw in the Western metaphysics of presence; but this aporia, this product of an apprehension of the gap between being and meaning, is the occasion of that work of symbolization that converts nature into culture and makes it both useful and valuable in the process. If there were no gap between being and meaning, nature and culture, then symbolization would hardly be necessary to human life. But symbolization indubitably *is* necessary. Art, as the most self-conscious investigation of the process by which symbolization is effected, not only demonstrates this exigency, but in its constant revisions of its own operations constantly reminds us of how difficult it is to symbolize *perfectly*.

Notes

1. See Richard Rorty, *Philosophy and the Mirror of Nature* (Princeton: Princeton University Press, 1980), Ch. 4, on "Privileged Representations," and pp. 284–311, on the problem of reference. Rorty's article on "Relations, Internal and External," in *The Encyclopedia of Philosophy*, ed. Paul Edwards (New York and London: Free Press, 1967), 7: 125–33, provides a brief survey of the relationship between the problem of essences and the general position of relativism in epistemology.
2. See Jacques Derrida, "Structure, Sign, and Play in the Discourse of the Human Sciences," in *Writing and Difference*, trans. Alan Bass (Chicago: University of Chicago Press, 1978), Ch. 10.
3. See Hegel's discussion of the specific tasks of philosophy in his

Introduction to his "Smaller Logic," *The Logic of Hegel*, trans. William Wallace (1874: rpt. Darby, Pa.: Arden Library, 1979), and the first chapter of *The Phenomenology of Mind*, trans. J. B. Baillie (1910; rpt. New York: Harper and Row, 1967), on sense certainty.

4. Arthur C. Danto, "Artworks and Real Things," in Morris Philipson and Paul J. Gudel, eds., *Aesthetics Today* (New York: New American Library, 1980), pp. 322–36.

5. On the distinction between use value, exchange value, and "real" value, see Marx's opening chapter of *Capital* on "Commodities."

6. The distinction between manual and mental or imaginative labor is suggested most pointedly in *The German Ideology*, and it is not abandoned in any substantial way in the work of the so-called later period of Marx's evolution. Indeed, the distinction is necessary for Marx to be able to account for the fact that human beings, unlike animals, are able to produce the kind of "distorted" notions of reality met with in "ideologies."

7. The career of the notions distilled into the distinctions among signs, indices, and symbols is economically represented in Roland Barthes, *Elements of Semiology*, trans. Annette Lavers and Colin Smith (New York: Hill and Wang, 1968), Ch. 2.

8. Nelson Goodman, *Ways of Worldmaking* (Indianapolis and Cambridge: Hackett, 1978), esp. Chs. 6 and 7.

9. Jonathan Culler, *Structuralist Poetics: Structuralism, Linguistics, and the Study of Literature* (Ithaca: Cornell University Press, 1975), Ch. 3.

10. These are Goodman's terms.

11. Harold Bloom, *A Map of Misreading* (Oxford: Oxford University Press, 1975).

12. For a discussion of the issues involved, see Geoffrey Hartman, *Criticism in the Wilderness: The Study of Literature Today* (New Haven: Yale University Press, 1980).

13. The principal representatives of the various positions are now conveniently anthologized in Susan R. Suleiman and Inge Crosman, eds., *The Reader in the Text: Essays on Audience and Interpretation* (Princeton: Princeton University Press, 1980).

14. I cannot resist using this occasion to recommend S. Giedion, *The Eternal Present: A Contribution on Constancy and Change*, Bollingen Series 35.6.1 (New York: Pantheon, 1962), with its superb

reproductions of cave art and the usual provocative insights of this great historian of culture.

15. On signature, see Goodman, *Ways of Worldmaking*, Ch. 2, and Richard Wollheim, "Pictorial Style: Two Views," in Berel Lang, ed., *The Concept of Style* (Philadelphia: University of Pennsylvania Press, 1979), pp. 129–45.

16. E. H. Gombrich, *Art and Illusion: A Study in the Psychology of Pictorial Representation* (Princeton: Princeton University Press, 1960), Chs. 3 and 4.

17. I owe this formulation to reflection on the work of Michael Fried, especially his article "Manet's Sources: Aspects of his Art, 1859–1865," *Artforum*, March 1969, pp. 28–82. See now Fried, *Absorption and Theatricality: Painting and Beholder in the Age of Diderot* (Berkeley and Los Angeles: University of California Press, 1980), the scope of which is much greater than its title indicates.

18. Claude Lévi-Strauss, *The Elementary Structures of Kinship*, trans. James Harle Bell et al. (Boston: Beacon Press, 1969), Ch. 2.

19. Ibid., Ch. 5.

20. See Berel Lang, "Towards a Poetics of Philosophical Discourse," *The Monist* 63, no. 4 (October 1980): 445–64.

21. This is only a hunch, based on the care which Derrida lavishes on Jabès' work. See Ch. 3 of *Writing and Difference*. This "care" is of a quite different, more solicitous kind than that employed in his usual "deconstructions."

22. For an example of the ways in which de Man appears to be deconstructing while engaged in the task of saving the literary work from reductionist impulses, see "Shelley Disfigured," in Harold Bloom et al., *Deconstruction and Criticism* (New York: Seabury, 1979), pp. 39–74. I take this anti-reductionist impulse to underlie and to authorize J. Hillis Miller's featuring of the figure of the *mis en abŷme* in his more recent work. For a defense of the "positivity" of deconstruction, see Miller, "The Critic as Host," ibid., esp. pp. 230–32.

Anna Balakian

Relativism in the Arts and the Road to the Absolute

It is incongruous for one as preoccupied as I have been for so many years with the pursuit of the "absolute" in poetry to write on relativism in the arts. In view of my approach to poetry in a consistently different direction, my response to relativist theories and praxis relating to the arts could well be flatly negative, in which case my work in poetry criticism would serve as the substantive basis of my argument. But I do not believe in deconstruction for its own sake as a purely dialectical exercise. This essay, therefore, will have two faces: one will involve the questioning of certain relativist attitudes, and the other an examination of positive alternatives which I have seen at work in modernism and which I believe to be viable within and despite the seemingly relativist climate of the era.

First, let me say candidly and without reservation that I do not believe in "creative criticism." Creativity in the arts propels the subjective consciousness on to a level of existence that can break away from the collective consensus about what is *real*, preferring to it what we consent to understand as *fiction*. Otherwise the subjectivity expressing itself in the field of the acceptable *real* would be not an artist but a reporter.

Ortega y Gasset made the distinction between levels of viewing the same phenomenon very clear in "A Few Drops of Phenomenology," the principal essay in his *Dehumanization of Art*.

In showing distinctions between the human being personally involved in a death—the reporter, the doctor, and the artist—he
observes a certain creative detachment on the part of the artist. I
would go further and suggest that there is a virtual severance on
the part of the artist from the phenomenon under observation.

The critic,[1] on the other hand, if a good one, is a supremely
efficient reporter who, as an intermediary between the artist and
the non-artist, creates a bridge between two distinct aspects of
human cognizance. To serve in that capacity of mediator, the
critic must also be something of a moralist; i.e., must possess an
a priori code of values against which he tests the *fiction* of the
creative artist and recasts it in terms of identifiable and differentiable components in regard to pre-established norms shared by
the non-artists. He must want to exercise *clarity* by showing
relations with the common reality, and to establish a new connection—where the link had been spliced—by focusing on the
deviations from reality which constitute the heart of that creativity. He cannot accomplish these two different functions of his
métier if he takes the point of view either of the non-artist or of
the artist. The critic's role is in the middle, between the secular
heaven of the artist and the earthly habitat of the non-artist. He
is in what Rilke would call the *Zwischenraum* with a voice neither of a god nor of a man. He is, to use Wallace Stevens's terminology, "the necessary angel."

If the critic, in the fashion of recent creatively inclined literary analysts, competes in intelligence and vision with the creator of the work perused, either he will overwhelm the work (as
in the case of Roland Barthes commenting on an inferior work
of Balzac in *S/Z*), or his commentary will emerge as a Xerox
copy of the initial work. In neither case will he have served the
role of critic as I have defined it; i.e., as a mediator.

If, on the other hand, the critic places himself squarely in the
crowd, becomes a non-differentiable receiver of the work, he

may simply be articulating the norm of receptions and become the dispensable reporter. It is in this second category of malfunctioning that the problems raised by the concept of relativism tend to miscarry the intentions and realizations of the created work.

In the late twentieth century there can be no questioning the fact that our world is relative to other worlds, our rainbow relative to other spectrums we know not of—to the light of "second suns," to use the imaginative language of the surrealist André Breton. We receive moonshine and give off earthshine to another globe. We are not a center of the universe, and, unlike Descartes or Kant, most of us no longer believe that whatever concepts we harbor about good, evil, justice, beauty, or truth were there somewhere in the heaven/sky before we came to discover and recognize them. By extension of this non-anthropocentric acceptance of relativism, the non-artist, without any assistance from the critic, could and does conclude more and more that he can thereby equally reject the condominium of artistic values and ignore the frontiers between art and non-art. Of course, this conclusion has a far-reaching effect on the democratization of the arts: everybody on his own terms can accept or reject anything as a work of art by giving his own interpretation of pleasure and meaning attributable to the object/work/image of contemplation. At that point the non-artist no longer needs a critic, and the critic who supports the premise of the critical autonomy of such readers/contemplators/beholders has ipso facto eliminated his own special function. Furthermore, the do-it-yourself concept of reception does away with classifications indicative of value judgments comparing one artist with another, but also determining the better or worse manifestations within the work of a single artist: *Sarrasine* is worth as much as *Le Père Goriot*, a letter written by Flaubert carries as much importance as a page from *Madame Bovary*! What has then disappeared along with the function of the critic is the concept of taste—which is an absolutist intrusion into the relativist world. Actually, today the value-laden word "avant-garde" has taken the place of taste as a director of aesthetic consciousness. If the theory of relativism were to go far enough to eliminate the inhibitions which prevent non-artists from rejecting what has been pre-rated as "avant-garde," these receivers of the work of art might well reject, in their general rebellion against taste, the non-critical acceptability of the "avant-garde" as a value. They might thereupon conclude that, if they do not like the profiles of Picasso or his bovine women, they may be permitted to cause mayhem with them, as Duchamp did with the Mona Lisa.

On the one hand, the elimination of the critic's code of values gives wide potential freedom of assessment to the receiver of the artifact who identifies himself as a critic at large operating under the guidelines of relativism. On the other hand, what happens to the individual who identifies himself as an artist, rather than as a viewer or a beholder, and who also carries into the world of art the relativist concept of the world of material reality? It would appear to such a person that if the relativist comprehension of the real world is applied to the comprehension of the art world, then it must follow that, to communicate with persons of such apperceptions, the artist can name anything an art object acceptable to receivers no longer guided by a priori tastes of the collective tradition or of the critic's judgment. If such is the case, the artist need no longer be sensitive to the distinction between the world of measurable reality and the *fiction* world created by artists, in the global sense of the word "artist." In that instance, the transformation of the critic into a reporter can be extended to the artist-person; for he has also become a reporter, identifying himself with the measurable entities of the universe. Having eliminated the differential of art, we have thereby eliminated the mediator who showed the dif-

ference, and we have also eliminated the artists, who constituted that distinct and separate category of persons. Anything
can presumably be art if it can solicit interpretation, and anyone
can thereby be an artist if he can persuade someone to interpret
his work. In this pseudo-utopia all persons are potentially artists,
since anything can be called an artifact as long as someone can
so "interpret" it.

The great fallacy is, of course, the presumption that interpretation of an artifact makes of it a work of art. The age of collage
is the product of a substratum of belief that entities can be related at random since, in the total schema of the cosmos, all are
condemned to remain ignorant of the whole. Just as the notion
of providence gave meaning to every act, so centrality gave meaning to every entity. On the contrary, randomness permits arbitrary choices of combinations of entities. Donald Kuspit says:
"Collage, for the first time in art, makes uncertainty a method
of creation, apparent indeterminacy a procedure." According to
Kuspit, then, we can find "the flotsam and jetsam of everyday
life set adrift in the collage,"[2] for, with collage, art is nowhere
and it is everywhere; it becomes a freewheeling way of dealing
with a random material, emblematic of fragmented experience.
Perhaps that is a working philosophy of living in the modern
world. It is indeed the basis of the obsession with the absurd,
according to which even acts of violence and assassinations have
no connection to a central emotion or belief. If the acceptance
of a gratuitous world destroys the design for living, that is the
business of each individual to determine in relation to his private life. But such personal choices do not eliminate, by the
same token, the premises upon which the distinction of art as a
separate sphere of existence survives.

Art, whether teleological, mimetic, or symbolic, cannot be
factored into the common denominator of the real world. Even
the recycling of ancient myths in modern literature is obvious

evidence that the diachronic connections point to a super-organization that functions independently and makes art immune to the caprices of natural reality. We could go so far as to say that the work of art is as different from the natural object as a fetus is from a cancerous growth: both organisms have cells developing inside the human structure, and those growing uncontrolled could presumably be called an aspect of human "creativity"; but one is an organized pattern, the other a random growth.

If uncertainty and indeterminacy are elements of the human condition highlighted in our modern world, they cannot filter into "modernism" without breaking essential rules of the art universe. In many statements made by writers working in the area of human consciousness rather than in literature and aesthetics, art is being equated with diverse practices of ambiguity. There is a marked difference between the open-ended interpretation of a piece of writing or an artifact according to relative values in an era no longer bound to an absolute code of aesthetics or ethics, and the diversity of interpretations caused by ambiguity of structure indicative of sloppy production. The defense of a "text" mysterious because of faulty, non-sustained design or execution on the basis of its compatibility with our random universe is a very weak defense.

There have been hermetic writings since the beginning of literature. The most eminent recent manifestation is the Symbolist aesthetics of the nineteenth century; its *art poétique* was precisely to construct an intentionally polysemantic network to provoke multiple interpretations and thus enrich the experience of the reader. Indeed I agree with Hayden White that works with the power of symbolization are of the highest level of artistic creativity. As he says: "The extent of its value as an artistic work is marked by the range of response that it induces as an object . . . of self-consciousness about the symbolizing process of which it is an instantiation, in its beholders."[3] But when a message is ambiguous because of inadequate composition, it becomes unacceptable as art, no matter how many interpretations are provoked by its amorphous structure.

Art, to be art, must have an organization, an intention. Even when tapping unconscious data it must at the same time attain support from the human powers of selectivity based on supremely conscious forces of concentration. It has become the fashion in recent criticism to frown upon studies of intentionalism. This attitude was a largely justified reaction, on the part of W. K. Wimsatt and Monroe C. Beardsley[4] and fellow critics of an earlier epoch, against the abuses of overemphasis on what an author was aiming to express, rather than what he did express. Such practices had led to an exaggerated stress on the study of peripheral documents in support of such intentions. But by now the pendulum has swung too far in the opposite direction. If it is indeed foolish to distract the reader from expressed meaning to intended meaning, it is on the other hand a flagrant injury to the artist to disregard, and even to go as far as to contradict, his intentions. In his article "Appreciation and Interpretation of Works of Art," Arthur Danto has the courage to argue that in interpreting a work of art we should not consider the intentions of the author extraneous to our understanding of the work: "I believe we cannot be deeply wrong if we suppose that the correct interpretation of object-as-artwork is the one which coincides most closely with the artist's own interpretation."[5]

When the sincere artist is expressing his intentions, he is not writing up a proposal for funding which may or may not be implemented! He is analyzing his creative process, which is an integral part of his art. He is measuring his potential, estimating his reach. He is making audible his inner struggle, staking the foundations of his edifice. I am convinced that we would not appreciate Rimbaud's *Illuminations* as we do if we did not also read the famous "letter of the seer" which he wrote to his teacher. In fact, his prose poems collected under the title of *Illuminations*, printed in random fashion in the Symbolist magazine *La Vogue* in 1886, and even subsequently collected in a volume, did not make a particular stir until the famous letter was published in 1912, putting the poems in perspective as part of an intended design.

The discussion of process and intentionality is part of the organization of the work of art, the building of an absolute world having its total autonomy under the control of its own god, the artist. He spells out its values, its hierarchy, the relative functions within an integrated whole, satisfying his own and his readers' holistic yearnings.

If the human receiver or beholder of the work of art can survive in a random cosmos (we wonder for how long!), it is because he has come out of the organized process of the fetus, which has given him an inherent model for the process of organization—and no one challenges or tries to deconstruct that natural process of organization. In fact, those scientists who emphasize the quantum theory, the mathematics of probabilities, and biological haphazardness, and those non-scientists who conclude from these assertions that the whole of existence is gratuitous and random are practicing the fallacy of partial truth. If there is an appreciable degree of unpredictability in nature, there are also strict, impeccable timetables of organization such as the development of the unit of life and the cycle of the seasons, not to mention the rotation of the earth around the sun. The organization of the artist deserves the same respect as do nature's organizations. Anyone tampering with the artist's network (such as quoting out of context or psychoanalyzing it according to norms established after and outside of its coded systems) is threatening that survival.

Art is an ontological alternative to religion. In fact, I noticed with some sense of déjà vu in rereading recently Jacques Maritain's *Frontiers of Poetry* that Maritain was apprehensive about the modern poet's extreme dedication to the creation of an absolute, fictitious existence. Of course, what he called "modern" was turn-of-the-century and early twentieth-century French poetry. Scrutinizing a tendency toward what, as a theologian, he would call "mystic" objectives in artists who otherwise avowed no religious inclinations, he was uncomfortable with certain of their postulations. In their search for an absolute without God, he, as a man of religion, feared that they might become confused about the poetic absolute and the teleological one. Maritain warned such artists that they might be venturing upon dangerous territory unless they were willing to surrender the poetic for the mystic. But most modern artists who grope for the absolute are not worried about such transgressions; even when they evoke medieval mystics, they secularize them.[6]

That there is a distinct and universally recognized gap between natural reality and the absolute world of the artist can most easily be tested by the fact that receiver-persons least sensitive to artworks can nonetheless distinguish without hesitation between what is life and what is a representative creation of life. In support of the theory that there is a more and more apparent trend toward the non-distinction between natural reality and art reality, critics point to that most notorious of examples, the urinal of Marcel Duchamp. Duchamp presumably made the daring leap, crossed the barrier, breached the gap. The essential point overlooked is the *manner*, the tone in which the urinal was offered as an artifact. Duchamp's *Fountain*-urinal was a manifesto, as was the moustache put on the Mona Lisa. It was a protest, a deconstructive act, bringing attention to what, to him, was a need to change a superannuated code of art, the very definition of the beautiful,[7] which sent him in search of ready-mades. He never intended it to be mistaken for an artwork in itself. It meant to him what the revolver shot meant to André Breton in his *Second Manifesto*: a call to arms, a provocation, a challenge not to disorder but to reorganization, to the creation of new designs.

In this connection the role of the so-called unconscious must be called into question. Since the turn of the century artists have been said to make efforts to incorporate the givens of the subconscious into art. Automatic writing is a case in point. The harvest of automatic writing was considered by André Breton as a supreme gift that life bestowed on the artist from the depth of its mysterious natural resources, but neither he nor coartists such as Soupault, Eluard, Dali, or Miró, equated the disorganized data of the unconscious with art. In Breton's vocabulary, automatism is a factor; but another word follows ever in its traces, and that word is "vigilance." The unconscious can only be funneled into art if it is monitored by vigilance, which controls its randomness. Even the earliest enthusiasts of modern psychology, such as James Joyce, were cautious of the uses of stream of consciousness. Molly Bloom's monologue is not a replay of a taped random discourse. And Proust's so-called involuntary remembrances are artistic subterfuges. Let us not for a moment be fooled into thinking that the madeleine dipped into the cup of tea acted like a magic wand to recapture a long-lost reality and give it a verbal reincarnation as a natural, and spontaneous matter of consequence. Perhaps a luminous moment was sparked, but Proust's reconstruction of the absolute world of the artist from the relative world of his memory was not an instant handout. To equate the Proustian childhood with the synthetic one he names and creates in his aesthetic search[8] is as naive as a recent researcher's slide collection of Valéry's native town of Sète, offered as an aid in the effort to capture the reality of "Le Cimetière marin."

Currently, the critic is more often guilty of pursuing the non-distinction between life and art than are the non-professional readers or viewers of the arts. The deliberate confusion currently perpetrated between the relative world in which we live and the absolute world in which art is nurtured and functions leads to a methodology of criticism that may well accelerate the demise of the arts. Sociology, psychoanalysis, linguistics, and philosophy have all adjusted their optic to a revision whereby the rejection of the absolute has been expressed by a reedited terminology. It determines and evaluates phenomena which, emptied of previous assumptions of autonomous codes, can now be interpreted according to newer concepts (no longer definitive) of life, time, space, and human responses. Now the critic, following the line of these inquiries into life, freed of absolutism, attempts to apply the language of inquiry to a domain which, in order to prevail, must maintain its yearning for the absolute (even in its current form of immanence rather than transcendence) as its sine qua non. It has been said that the new critic deconstructs linguistic codes that are prejudicial to the meanings inherent in the basic structures of the text-artifact. I would suggest that most often he succeeds in deconstructing the organization of the work of art itself, rather than the supposed residue of prejudices. For instance, in defining "symbol" Paul Ricoeur talks of "surplus of signification," thereby failing to distinguish between the nature of art and the nature of life. In nature's wilderness there are surpluses of weeds; in the good gardener's terrain there are no surpluses, because nature's surpluses have been weeded out. Even so, when a viewer measures the work of art on a relative scale of less, adequate, too much and feels a "surplus," he is blind to the basic substance of artistic value. There is no surplus in the absolute totality of the work of art.

But if relativism is the inevitable philosophy of the age, is it driving modern man in a direction where art cannot follow? Or must art follow at the risk of losing its intrinsic differential? Must it run that risk, rather than cease to be a need in human life? My position is that the situation calls for neither resistance nor capitulation to relativism. There are ways of accommodating to it without identifying relativism as a basis for a new concept of the arts. It is one thing to view the artifact from the adjusted vantage point of a relativist optic, and quite a different thing to transplant artificially the relativist optic *into* the work of art.

Esoteric writers such as Mallarmé, Rimbaud, and Yeats and reticent ones such as neoclassicists have been the victims of the kind of interpretation that substitutes for their absolute codes certain relativist, permissive ones culled from recent ideologies. Synchronic approaches to their works rob them of their pristine meanings by suggesting that arbitrary meanings may be read into them. The process turns the work of art into a "text" or document, bringing it out of the absolute realm of the artist into the relativist one of the critic who has retreated from his intermediary stance back into the world of those for whom he presumably interprets.

But, one might ask, what is the alternative? In reading Rimbaud or gazing upon an El Greco, must our objective be simply to become aware of the breach, of the distance between our comprehension of the universe and theirs? In ages when real life was controlled by absolute values, as was the world of artists, the correspondence between life and its representation in the arts was easier. Of course, there is the danger that, if we can kill art by imposing on it a relativity incompatible with its intrinsic nature, we can also destroy it by increasing the gap between life as we now understand it and art, thus producing a diminution and eventual absence of communication between the two. I must concede that the current use of tools inappropriate to the decoding of art is, in a sense, prompted by the desire to find a level of communication between the artist and his search for reception. But this objective can be accomplished without violating the intention or meaning of the work of art. We can engage in comparative approaches, rather than artificially impose a process of identification.

Take, for instance, the matter of point of view in narrative: it is a question that has become almost an obsession of literary analysts these days. By contrast, most novelists were not overtly concerned with the problem until recently, and even in the twentieth century it has not been a major preoccupation for many of the most renowned writers. Modern psychologists, on the other hand—and legally oriented detective-story writers— have made current readers very sensitive to the process of detection of point of view and the relative interpretations of behavior such variations can bring about, bearing directly on determinations of truth, sincerity, deceit. As a result of such interest, works of art are reexamined to point out the "fallacies" in the apperceptions of omniscient writers and viewers subjected to disparate points of view. Awareness of this mechanism of point of view encouraged by a relativist attitude causes the critic to impose heavy burdens on works whose authors made no issue of this element of novel structure. The classic example is Sartre's article on François Mauriac,[9] in which he accuses the novelist of playing God by knowing, contrary to the rule of plausibility, the workings of several minds at the same time. Mauriac is accused, consequently, of creating a predictability of behaviors that may be in the power of gods to effect but that would confound psychologists. What Sartre overlooks is the fact that Mauriac's fictitious world does not consist of casebook histories; rather, it is his own private property, controlled not by laws handed down by Moses but according to the options of the creator of the novel. If Sartre wants to enter Mauriac's universe as a reader, he must accept the rules of Mauriac's game—or, having acknowledged that those rules are different from those he practices in the world of reality, he has the choice of comparing his world with Mauriac's artistic one, and thus exercising his role as a mediator. What he is not called upon to do is to impose *his* reality upon Mauriac's, and then chastise him for breaking his own (Sartre's) set of rules.

There has been controversy over critical methodologies and attitudes to which the notion of creativity is central. Because the barriers between genres have been lowered, and the separations between media have been bridged by what is known as multimedia artifacts, does this phenomenon justify the infringement of the critic upon the realm of creativity? Many are taking a free-trade attitude, admitting the permissive character of art by all and for everybody's sake. I have no quarrel with anyone who wants to call his shoe a work of art, but I dare any critic to redescribe René Magritte's *Le Modèle rouge* in such a way that it can fit his lower extremity and serve him in the act of walking. That he may create his own model is his own business, but that he may infringe on some other person's model simply means, in critical (as in political) terminology, that he is usurping the absolute authority of the proprietor over his own domain.

Of course, it is far easier to protest than to predicate, and the second part of this essay will prove that point by being much shorter. My focus so far has been on the behavior of the critic committed to relativism; my observation has been of the realm of the existing artworks, most of which through the generations of Western culture are the product of an absolute universe. Now let us turn to the artist himself, as he stands today on the shifting sands, passing from absolute codes to relative ones in the realm of human behavior. Let us observe how the change has affected the search for the absolute in the domain of the arts. How have artists coped with the situation and, further, how can we suggest that they cope with it? Are they ready to decontrol art and surrender it to life? Or can they proceed as if nothing has happened? Is there a third alternative in trying to represent the relativist attitude toward life within the context of a controlled artifact? Artists have been answering "yes" to all three questions. Some have indeed abandoned the distinction between life and art: the makers of found poetry, concrete art, happenings, autobiographies that are in fact a collage of taped automatic discourses interspersed with strips of fantasy. I would be loath to call the authors of such productions "artists" unless I could find a conscious principle of composition consistently observed throughout their work. There are also those who, according to their own codes, reflect or represent the random universe. Samuel Beckett is a past master of the art of representing the absurd character of the cosmos, but in reading him we are not meant to attribute to Molloy or Moran anything but a fictitious existence. It has been a critical fallacy to identify the personal philosophy of artists such as Beckett or Camus or Sartre with the attitudes of characters they have created to fit into contrived social contexts in which the gratuitous is heavily stacked.

In this respect, it is interesting to examine J. Hillis Miller's article about Faulkner's *Absalom, Absalom!*[10] He examines evidence of what might be judged to be (but is not) faulty construction in Faulkner's narration techniques involving vacillations in point of view and repetitions of narrations, both of which suggest an ambiguity of design. Then he explains that these ambiguities correspond to the lack of design in the lives of real-life characters. Normally, he says, storytellers "go beyond mimesis, to create something which is one degree or another a fiction not wholly grounded in its exact correspondence to things as they are." In the case of Faulkner he finds that the author desists from "making something happen" out of noncohesive facts of the reality he has observed. In other words, he effects an "analogy between the failure of a design in life and the failure of narration." Miller proposes that "this failure of a narration is, for Faulkner, the evidence of its validity, since only the failed narration, which exposes its loose ends and inconsistencies, can be an adequate representation." He concludes that, in its very failure "as coherent design," Faulkner's novel finds its ultimate design "which is to give knowledge, however indirect and fleeting, not of the facts of history or of life, but of the enigmatic power behind these." In this extremely subtle analysis which ascertains the process of Faulkner's deliberate ambiguity, Miller is suggesting that the closer observation of life and the subordination of the natural instinct of the artist to put order in the disorder, and coherence into the randomness of life, have indeed brought Faulkner into closer correspondence with mimesis, not through reportage (as it would have been in the case of avowed naturalists) but by accommodation of the creative process to the natural storytelling process. He shows his confidence in Faulkner's techniques of composition when, step by step, he demonstrates the deliberate elements of ambiguity by which Faulkner suggests the ambivalence of life itself. The work of Faulkner is "ambiguous," then, only to the logical mind viewing the work of art according to rules applicable to a documentary. It is highly compatible with the artist's interpretation of the nature of human existence.

So far, the analysis of Faulkner's intentions and creative success in seeming failure holds together convincingly. But as a mediator between the reader and the artist, perhaps the critic can go one step further in the analysis of indeterminacy. We could suggest that documentary reportage can also convey the inconsistencies of human behavior. How do we differentiate between the documentary text communicating the inconsistencies of behavior and a work of art having the same objectives? I would argue that, in assessing ambiguities in the work of art, three dimensions should be considered by the critic as I have earlier defined him in the role of mediator. We have to discover whether the ambiguities have occurred because of faulty organization and composition, or whether they have been prompted by a desire for a greater approximation of reality (approaching, indeed, the structure of a documentary). Miller's explanation in the case of *Absalom, Absalom!* leans toward this second form of ambiguity. But the communication of ambiguities can also become part and parcel of a new form of artistic construction rejecting the mimetic for the artificial; in this case the artist persuades us to accept the contrived defaults of narration as a system of correspondences with human indeterminacy. In the course of this process he raises our vision to a level of creative fiction where these indeterminacies become acceptable to us. This process is more frequent in poetry than in prose. For instance, in Yeats the golden bird of Byzantium is a permanent existence although not a real one, situated in a location lifted by the artist out of passing historicity. In questioning the degree and manner of the artifice and the artist's control of the relative factors, the mediator has a valid basis for evaluating the quality of the work of art— not in terms of its current relevance to the relativist optic, any more than in terms of a teleological preestablished code of values, but according to his ability to be consistent in the manipulation of inconsistencies intentionally implanted in the artifact.

The development of creative ambiguity as the artist's response to the compounding of indeterminacy in cosmic and human movement was indeed the basis of Symbolist aesthetics, of which Mallarmé was the most notable and conscious master. In his aesthetics of ambiguity Mallarmé was not accommodating to relativism (which, as a thoroughly avowed agnostic, he accepted) but competing with it. In techniques that are very consistent, very precise and unambiguous, he developed an art of ambiguity to suggest on the artist's own terms the questionable human condition among dead constellations and blind paths and unexpected collisions in unguided vessels and in undirected courses. Hermeneutic criticism that produces exegesis to solve unilaterally the riddle of these symbolist poetic structures is a reductive process which actually transforms the creative simulation of relativism into a form of absolute meaning. A critical approach that would be much more relevant to the spirit of Symbolist *écriture* is the study of the artistic process and the identification of the components which succeed (and in some cases fail) to suggest the uncertainty of phenomena and the plurality of meaning (not surplus).

But the response to relativism which I would predicate, in lieu of the abdication of the absolute or the simulation of the relative with the controlled tools of the artist, is the attitude of certain moderns who, in the face of relativity of values and randomness of phenomena, cling the more closely to that world of the arts where they can create their own code and maneuver as they please, according to their own creative systems. They do not, as of old, latch onto a supernal organization; rather, in their longing for an absolute, they reinterpret the sacred in human terms and through human form.

The revised definition of "sacred" means essentially immunization from interference, possession of its own sacrament, a system of symbolization of which the correspondences are strictly intramural or self-referential to start and become intermural only when other artists accept the signal-making character of the work, a sign of the seminal power and "greatness" in the recycled definition of the word. It is "influence" in its most creative, transformational sense, and it was the basis of the remarkable spread of Symbolist poetry. The symbols that Mallarmé generated related to each other, and he indicated the role of the reader as an interpreter. The mediation was to be an internal one barring infringement from the external world. In that sense *Hérodiade* is an achievement of process, whereas *The Afternoon of a*

Faun is a meditation on process. *Hérodiade* is the self-contained universe of the artist as represented by the enclosure in which the princess lives; the commentary of the nurse could be likened to critical interpretation which, in its effort to associate Hérodiade with the outside world, has no relevance to the enclosure. When the nurse touches Hérodiade's hair, her repulsion is that of the artist attacked by forces outside itself. The myth of Salome itself had become so common in the era that it had lost its autonomy in relation to the ordinary world, and by substituting the name Hérodiade for Salome, Mallarmé was making a revision—an effort to reconstruct the fiction itself, which had deviated into the mire of ordinary reality and lost the distance from it which a true myth usually preserves.

It is often pointed out that the Surrealists broke with the cloistered world of the nineteenth-century aesthetes to return to the world of daily existence and to utilize it in poetic communication. The conclusion drawn from such a general statement might well be that, more than any previous group, they had arrived at the non-distinction between the real and the artistic. Had not André Breton stated in *Surrealism and Painting* that the surreal resides in the real? But he did not thereby equate the one with the other. The surrealists took the trouble to explain more explicitly than any previous coterie the process of transformation from the real to the artifact, precisely because of their awareness that the problem of relativism and its connections with the poet ("poet" taken in the broad sense of the word, encompassing the painter as well) was of more direct and urgent concern than it had ever been considered before.

The primary objective in the case of the surrealists was to recuperate the random and the senseless, the automatic and the fortuitous, and to introduce these elements into a controlled universe through the monitoring of the activity of the imagination, which in Breton's definition becomes a powerhouse of creativity. The rebus-type of poetic/plastic imagery utilized by ancient Kabbalists to suggest the hermetic character of a meaningful universe was appropriated as a central form of cognition and communication in surrealist writing and art, to convert the ambiguity of the void-cosmos into a multiplicity of desires named/ consummated by the creative power of the poet/painter. This form of creative writing or painting predicates that nature's indifferent chance-mechanism can be channeled to satisfy human intentions, that disparate existences found in natural reality can be aligned into coherent correspondences in a universe in which the artifacts produce interrelationships.

Pascal's accommodation to human frailty was grounded in the proposition that the intellect's power to recognize physical mortality in a universe whose purposes were hidden from man gave him a certain power over the forces of darkness. We find in surrealist doctrine a total philosophic reversal: man's power over his ephemeral existence resides in his ability to engender purpose *where there is none*, placing a value on human creativity higher than that of a blind nature which gains its visibility through the artifact. American intellectuals interested in problems of relativism as it affects modernism should study the works of André Breton more closely than they have up to now. Breton tackled the fundamental problem of our era and, in large measure, learned to cope with it: how to preserve the power and dignity of the artist in a teleologically undermined cosmos. He provided a philosophical basis to the need to revise notions of beauty in order to preserve beauty from total extinction. He set new norms for the quest for the absolute without naive displays of adherence to superannuated structures. His was not the secular humanism of classic vintage that placed man at the center of the *existing* universe—against which much of modernism protests. Instead, he made a broad-based appeal to the artist to confirm his centrality in the universe of the artifact, in the face of an admittedly non-anthropocentric universe.

In an article called "The Death of the Author," included in a collection characteristically called *The Discontinuous Universe*, Roland Barthes attempts to wrench the work of art from the control of its author and to surrender it to the caprices of the reader. He tells us that "a text is not in its origin, it is in its destination, but this destination can no longer be personal: the reader is a man without history, without biography, without psychology; he is only that *someone* who holds gathered into a single field all the paths of which the text is constituted."[11] I find this statement not only fallacious but perverse, reflecting Barthes' warped, twisted notion of collectivism.

Unity is organization; without a directed construct there would be, as I have attempted to demonstrate, no act of creation. Such a "text" would be worthy only of biopsy, not of appreciation or inspiration or desire for comprehension. After dispossessing the creator of the "text," Barthes proceeds to disown the reader by declaring him anonymous, non-historical, a-psychological, in fact a monster from outer space. What he is probably trying to say obliquely is that many influences form a writer, and that these influences are amalgamated into his writings, to be perceived by future readers of diverse formations; no particular message can be handed down from one author to all readers in this relative world of fluctuating meanings. We could argue that, by the very negatively expressed manner of his statement, he transforms a truism into a demolition of the creative function, robbing it of individuality, stifling it in ambiguity, and making it the target of an impersonal, amorphous reception on the part of an equally ambiguous, featureless humanity. If the emphasis on the word "without" is meant to suggest, in its negation of the specific, a multiplicity and diversity of receptions, the meaning is colored by a language that attributes to the human creature a dismembered, disconnected character, the better to underline the discontinuity with which he, Barthes, is himself obsessed. It delivers art into the stream of spatial floating. Theories of relativity applied to the arts have given Barthes an excuse for the devalorization of Western culture without offering an alternative. Other post-Sartrian pessimists have taken the same line of dogmatic postulations; for example, Derrida's disquieting attacks on referentiality, perception, and valorization in any form. The didacticism of the critic is projected onto the work of art, as evidenced in a quotation from Jack Burnham's "Systems Esthetics": "The specific function of modern didactic art has been to show that art does not reside in material entities, but in relations between people and between people and the components of their environment." [12] Such a statement evokes cognitive disciplines, rather than the activities in the field of the arts.

It seems to me that, more than ever before, it is imperative to gear to full capacity the power of the artistic imagination to combat the increasingly amorphous appearance of the world in which the human species finds itself. As individual performance and affirmation become more and more difficult in a society where we are bunched together in a state which Beckett calls "namelessness," the dominion of the artist over the fictitious world of his creation needs to be guarded both against the tools of inquiry intended for the comprehension of the material universe and against assessments on a scale of relative values from which the classification as "art" excludes it categorically.

The demise of absolute values may make the universe collapse, as perceived by Beckett's character Molloy: "I listen and the voice is of a world collapsing endlessly." Beckett describes what man might become under an indifferent sky, like Moran "ready to go without knowing where he was going consulting neither map nor timetable." But when Beckett writes of "anguish of vagrancy and freedom" he is talking of ordinary *Homo* not so *sapiens*, not of the artist. In highly Christian periods the arts were known to reinforce the spiritual concepts of the absolute. We can no longer expect that, but in the current a-centric era the survival of any semblance of the arts depends on the artist's assumption of a role of leadership in a domain abandoned by its previous proprietors. The undermining of the spiritual absolute under the weight of evidences of relativity as a controlling factor of the universe calls for retaliation. We have drifted too long in the interregnum which Mallarmé declared almost a hundred years ago. Survivors of the millennium cannot abide in the sites of deconstruction; they must forge ahead. They cannot be expected to respond to pretentious simulations of a gratuitous universe by splashes of paint on canvas and the juggling of words on paper in the name of "art." There has to come a point when "post" becomes "pre," when late-night is recognized as pre-dawn.

Notes

1. If I am to pronounce myself on relativism, I have to do it as a critic and first define that role as I see it in relation to the general reader and the creative writer.
2. Donald B. Kuspit, "Collage: The Organizing Principle of Art in the Age of the Relativity of Art," in this volume.
3. Hayden White, "The Limits of Relativism in the Arts," in this volume.
4. William K. Wimsatt, *The Verbal Icon: Studies in the Meaning of Poetry* (Lexington: University Press of Kentucky, 1954).
5. Arthur C. Danto, "The Appreciation and Interpretation of Works of Art," in this volume.
6. Such was the objective of André Breton in his search for process

in the alchemical writers of the Middle Ages, among them Nicolas Flamel and Abraham the Jew; he shared no religious beliefs with them.

7. Cf. Aragon, *Anicet,* for the parody of the search for the new beauty.

8. Let us not overlook the fact that the word Proust used was *recherche* and not *souvenir*—an active, creative search, and not a passive reception. Why the translators continue to use the wrong word escapes my understanding!

9. Jean-Paul Sartre, *Situations,* I (Paris: Gallimard, 1947).

10. J. Hillis Miller, "The Two Relativisms: Point of View and Indeterminacy in the Novel," in this volume.

11. Roland Barthes, "The Death of the Author," in *The Discontinuous Universe,* ed. Sallie Sears and Georgianna W. Lord (New York: Basic Books, Inc., 1972), p. 12.

12. Jack Burnham, *Great Western Salt Works* (New York: George Braziller, 1974), p. 16.

Elliott Schwartz   **Performance**
                          in the Midst of
                          Pluralism

Although I have been asked to comment here upon some aspects of relativism in the arts, I must confess that I never use the
word "relativism," and I'm not really sure that I know what it
means. But I certainly use the word "relative"; I apply it to that
which is not "absolute." So far, so good: if we can be sure of
anything in the world of twentieth-century art, it is the absence
of absolutes. Virtually no certainties remain for the creative artist; the crossing of boundaries, confusion of categories, and re-
definitions of limits that used to characterize the work of a few
hardy, outrageously avant-garde souls are now familiar challenges (or problems, or crises) for us *all*. In that sense, the use
of the word "relativism" in a discussion of contemporary art is
apt.

   On another level, however, I find the term problematic, and
perhaps a bit loaded. Things or (more likely) qualities are usually considered "relative" with respect to *others* of like nature,
often in implicit comparison along a sliding scale or continuum. For example, the attributes of "heat" and "cold" are relative descriptions of the same phenomenon: a given temperature.
We can also describe comparative altitudes as "higher" or "lower."
I am not sure, though, that the many conflicting and often contradictory philosophies, techniques, and habits that people apply
to the creation (or even the perception) of art are "relative" in

this way. That is, today's great variety of styles and definitions would make any simple comparison absurd; perhaps we shouldn't even attempt to find a common ground, mutually held assumptions, or connections—*relationships*, hierarchical or otherwise—in any of this vast multiplicity. To whatever extent the term "relativism" suggests relationships, I become skeptical. My instinctive response is an overwhelming desire to substitute a different term: "pluralism," which (for me) conveys in an objective, non-judgmental way the fact that we now inhabit an artistic milieu of many separate, equal, and independent options.

But wait again. There is still another way of interpreting the term "relative" as applied to the state of contemporary art. That other interpretation resonates with overtones of despair, frustration, bewilderment: the resigned admission, on the part of those whose certainties have been betrayed, that it's all "*only* relative"—that values, standards, and boundaries have become so debased that they are now trivial. After all, exclaim those who feel most betrayed, where are beauty, nobility of purpose, and the aesthetic experience in a world where not a single value is fixed? How can we tell whether a given object or experience is supposed to be a work of music, or painting, or dance, or architecture, or poetry? How do we know if it's art or non-art? And how do we know if it's any *good*? Are we the only ones who care about such things? (If so, are these questions worth asking?) In this sense, "relativism" may well represent a kind of nightmare for those who once loved art—art as they defined it—very deeply.

Certainly in my own field of music there has been a widespread reexamination (some would say abandonment) of all traditionally fixed definitions and values. Until the twentieth century, Western art music was bounded by a number of fairly stable traditions. Composers, performers, and listeners could assume the existence of a European mainstream, admittedly with its various national tributaries, within which many values were unquestioned. It was assumed, for example, that the logic of pitch relationships dominated all other considerations. Pitch itself was defined rather narrowly, in terms of the twelve more or less equal divisions of the octave. By the mid-eighteenth century, the goal-centered grammar of tonality had come to dominate the ways in which these twelve pitches could be combined, successively or simultaneously. In fact, tonal relationships became the chief means for articulating form *and* content, expressivity *and* structure, at the macro- *and* the micro-levels, all at once. As dense polyphonic textures had evolved over the centuries, a complex notational system of fairly high specificity (at least with regard to synchronization) had evolved as well. By the nineteenth century it was generally assumed that a musical score's function was to be as specific as possible, that a performer's most obvious responsibility was the faithful realization of every detail in that score, and that in many important respects the score *was* the "work." Performance was a representation—inevitably an imperfect one—of the immutable facts of the notated score.

Such assumptions were related to other beliefs of a more general nature—about the role of music in society, the "expressive" power of musical gestures, music as the articulation of an individual's "statement" or "argument," and the concert as a self-sufficient ritual activity. (The latter two were inextricably bound to the dominance of goal-centered tonality, the evolution of the large sonata-cycle format for Western instrumental music, and the obsessive concern that music always be "interesting.") All of these assumptions taken together, at their greatest extreme, would suggest a caricature of German music rather than of French or Italian, or of instrumental music rather than of vocal. But some or all of these assumptions, in greater or lesser degree, operated throughout Europe from the eighteenth century on. They constitute what we might call the Western tradition.

Today, we find *no* single tradition functioning with the same single-minded assurance. Rather, the musical community of composers, performers, and listeners is continually faced with choices among many traditions: alternative ways of thinking about

Intonation/Inflection
Pitch
Scale/Goals
Time/Motion
Texture
Volume

which are the surface results of more fundamental, deep-seated attitudes about

Logic/Order
Responsibility
Interest
Expressivity
High Purposes

and which, finally, come down to the most basic issues of all,

Music as "activity" or as "object"
The roles of creator, performer, and listener
Music's function/social rituals, spaces, and occasions for
    music.

This great range of options is the direct result of our increased knowledge of other cultures, a knowledge that we have acquired by travel, reading, and the use of recordings. (Recording technology has, in addition, created a new subculture and "tradition" of its own, if only because many basic issues must be redefined in a society that perceives music primarily via loudspeakers or headphones. We will return to this subject later on.)

As we avail ourselves of these options, we should note that a number of the above choices—even conflicting or apparently contradictory ones—can be adopted at the same time, or picked up and discarded in rapid succession. That is, stylistic consistency is no longer necessarily a virtue. On the contrary, artistic eclecticism often seems preferable to earlier ideals of "system" or "logic." We might even argue that an eclectic approach produces a new kind of open system, or a collage of overlapping systems, with its own freewheeling logic. And if that is so—if a certain sense, a pattern (even an ever-shifting one) is discernible amidst all this creative multiplicity—then perhaps the term "relativism" does have some pertinence for this discussion.

I suspect that this freewheeling sort of logic does exist. And whether we perceive today's artistic world as "relativistic" or "pluralistic," I believe (despite my earlier protestations!) that we can find some common concerns and related ways of thinking throughout that world. I would like to touch on two of these concerns, particularly as they apply to composers: (1) the area of *performance*, in the light of expanded roles and changing technology, and (2) a heightened awareness of *multiplicity* itself, the special sensibility—perhaps a new kind of "courage"—that allows one to cope with an overload of alternatives and the absence of imposed certainties.

Performance is perhaps the only certainty we have in music. In many of the world's cultures music exists solely by way of performance, without the intermediary of the notated score. Even within the Western concert tradition of the set "object" and its fixed relationships, performance is still considered necessary to bring that "object" to life. And those composers of our own time who are most concerned with carefully reasoned arguments and set relationships, such as the serialists, take performance options into account as well; a work designed for recording and loudspeaker transmission offers its composer challenges and opportunities different from one conceived with the concert hall in mind. Similarly, a composition being planned for electronic realization at the synthesizer is created differently, from the very start, from one intended for live, human performance. Finally (at the other end of the Western concert music spectrum), those composers who are more concerned with immediate, spontaneous activity than with fixed bits of information—followers of Cage rather than of Babbitt, to use a well-worn analogy of the '60s—are practically obsessed with performance considerations. Many of them have dedicated their creative lives not to the fashioning of "objects" at all, but to the shaping of performances.

On a different level, performance is integral to *all* the arts. A painter or sculptor engages in physical activity during the creation of a work; those of us who perceive the work must follow visual patterns with our eyes, or move around the sculpture, or walk about the picture gallery. These are all "performances." We may "perform" works of architecture by moving around and within them, or by reading blueprints (if we have the skill and imagination to decipher them). Similarly, we might "perform" music by making sounds with our voices or instruments, or by reading the printed score—or by placing a record on a turntable and causing loudspeakers to vibrate. In any of these situations we are absorbed in the creation or re-creation of an artwork, engaged in a ritual (public more often than private) which brings art to life. Composers have usually been concerned with the most immediate, obvious levels of performance related to their particular art: the use of voices or instruments to make sounds. But, in this peculiarly pluralistic age, they are beginning to consider other levels of performance as well.

Even at the most immediate, uncontroversial level of commonly defined musical "performance"—four people sitting down to play a string quartet, for example; or a pianist dealing with a lyric, expansive solo passage—complex factors and relationships are at work. As composers become more aware of these factors (I should amend that to "more *consciously* aware"—we have always intuitively recognized these), they find ways of stretching them, altering them, using them as positive stimuli for their creative work. Here are four such factors, essential to all performances everywhere.

(1) *Space*: physical, architectural, acoustical. A performance takes place not in the abstract, but in a setting: a small room, a large hall, a cathedral, a gymnasium, a chapel, town square, restaurant, and so on. Each of these spaces will have its own dimensions and will cause sound to reverberate and resonate in a unique way. In addition, each space offers special architectural challenges, visual reference points, and built-in cultural associations. These may influence the positioning of the musicians and the spectators (whether they stand, sit, or move; whether they all face in the same direction) and the general attitude that all bring to the activity at hand—which may *not* be exclusively that of music-making. In fact, throughout history we would be much more likely to find music being performed as one component of a larger ceremonial ritual (a lawn party, coronation, or religious observance, for example) than as a self-sufficient ritual of its own.

Composers have always taken performance space into consideration, perhaps with more conscious awareness regarding certain kinds of pieces (or during certain historical periods) than others. It is difficult to listen to Gregorian chant, for example, without recalling the resonances and echoes of a cathedral or monastery, the placement of singers, and even their movement during a religious ceremony. A Haydn string quartet was designed for performance in a rather large living room, a typical Mozart divertimento for outdoor entertainment, a typical Gabrieli canzona for antiphonal question-answer dialogue across the vast interior of San Marco in Venice, with the brass groups situated in balconies, boxes, or alcoves. Marches are usually conceived with outdoor performance in mind, plus the idea that the body of players—and perhaps listeners as well—will be in motion. The twentieth century has seen a great increase in pieces utilizing antiphonal separation of forces, from *The Unanswered Question* of Charles Ives to Henry Brant's many spatial works for various ensembles and Karlheinz Stockhausen's ventures for multiple orchestras surrounding the audience.

Our century has also witnessed the creation of an entirely new breed of performance space: the loudspeaker (or headphone set) which transmits electrically generated signals. The loudspeaker may be employed for the "performance" of music especially created for it—that is, music made in an electronic studio (taped, synthesized, or computer-generated) or studio recordings of rock/pop music designed for commercial sale and speaker transmission; the speakers can *also* be used to "perform" music which was, in fact, originally intended for different spaces, such as symphonies or string quartets. In the latter situation, interesting cross references and cultural mismatches can develop, especially since the loudspeaker not only functions as a performance space in its own right, but also converts its surroundings—which may be quite literally anywhere, from the interior of a car to one's kitchen, to a deserted beach, to a jet plane 35,000 feet in the air—into a wider "performance" area.

(2) *Objects* that occupy and dominate the space, or (of more immediate musical interest) *sounding bodies*: we usually refer to these as "instruments." To simplify matters, let us also consider the human voice as an instrument—a wind instrument, attached to another variety of sounding body.

We all know that composers are concerned about instruments and are usually quite careful in their choice of an instrument to articulate a certain passage in a particular work; we also might assume (correctly, most of the time) that such choices are dictated by matters of timbre. But instruments often dominate performances in ways that have little to do with their tone colors. (They may even control our attention by their silent presence on stage!) For one thing, instruments are fascinating, frequently beautiful "objects," impressive when simply viewed as sculpture or items of furniture. Certain visual images connected with instruments (the carving and painted lid of a harpsichord; light glancing off the polished brass of a horn; the weight and mass of grouped kettledrums) are literally unforgettable. They may complement or contradict the architectural setting in which they're placed. Certain instruments, such as the giant cathedral pipe organ, *are* part of the architecture. In this connection it is important to realize that many instruments have been designed for specific spaces. In the Middle Ages, instruments were frequently classified as "indoor" or "outdoor," depending upon their penchant for sweet, whispered voices or raucous, buzzing timbres. The organ of the Baroque is meant to resonate in a vast public space; the tiny clavichord in a very intimate, private one.

Beyond the fact that instruments are visually fascinating, they have the unique ability to force the humans who operate them into equally fascinating shapes. Observe the gestures and muscular operations—even contortions, at times—of anyone playing the piano, violin, trombone, or clarinet. The "dance" may be unintentional, but the sheer choreography is often brilliant. In fact, the entire physical relationship of human performer and inanimate object (instrument) is worthy of study. To consider but one dimension of that relationship, the differences in size between human and instrument may affect our perception of performance: the piccolo no larger than a chicken bone, for example, or the grand piano large enough to attack, overwhelm, and even devour its "tamer."

This last comment might lead one to think that instruments are somehow "alive," or that they possess magical powers. In other cultures, instruments are indeed regarded with a very special kind of awe; whatever the force is that can make a hollowed tree limb, or a construction of animal bones or hide, "speak" with a distinctive voice, it must be treated with respect. Similarly, instruments of the sophisticated Western tradition also have some of the attributes of living beings: distinctive personalities, as well as "biographies." The organ, for example, is not only an imposing physical object in space, but also a storehouse of memories, historical associations, and cultural relationships. A composer writing a work for organ might have any number of the following images flash by: a Bach chorale prelude (and the firm sound of the great German Baroque organ), Radio City Music Hall, a roller-skating rink, the French Romantic sound (and instrument) of Franck, soap-opera background music, a simple New England parlor, the "Phantom of the Opera" . . . and on and on. Some of those images and associations may, in fact, work their way into the new piece, if the composer finds them sufficiently powerful.

On another level, instruments may tell us a great deal about social history and changing taste. The piano is probably the most familiar object in Western music—or at least it was between 1750 and 1950, succeeding the lute and preceding the ascendancy of the electric guitar. Interestingly enough, the piano's construction stresses those attributes which dominated Western style during that period. The keyboard makes it easy to produce simultaneous sounds (chords) and is ideal for homophonic texture. In using the keyboard a performer creates individual pitches in neat, precise steps, since the piano's engineering has made it impossible to articulate pitches as glides, slides, swoops, vibrato, or any other "dirty" inflection. The pitches are also fixed in the unalterable series of twelve equally tempered steps to the octave. This tempered scale facilitated the modulations, transpositions, sequences, and complex key relationships—in fact, the entire tonal language—that generated the sonatas and symphonies of the Classic and Romantic periods.

It is childishly simple to coax a sound out of the piano: just depress a key. Compare this to the effort needed to make any kind of music on a violin or oboe. On the other hand, the piano poses the most extraordinary challenges at the most complex levels of fingerwork, multi-voiced polyphony, and dynamic control. (In trying to meet these challenges, a performer may also wind up looking quite glamorous and "romantic.") From all this we might gather that musical tastes during this period were increasingly dominated by the middle classes, who wanted simple amateur music for their own home entertainment but who also adored the sight of a sexy virtuoso stretching an instrument to its limits. We might also guess (correctly) that northern Europe had replaced the south as the center of musical power. Pianos are instruments designed for the interiors of well-insulated buildings; they stay indoors, and are therefore ideally suited for a society that generally stays indoors as well. (In more temperate regions where people move outside more frequently, hand-held instruments—such as the guitar—might have greater cultural force.)

I don't mean to suggest that composers, performers, or listeners are always consciously aware of any or all of these factors. But the sum total of considerations and associations surrounding performance space and sounding bodies must inevitably, at one level or another, influence the way composers create their music—and the way the rest of us perceive it.

(3) *Ritual*: the behavior that people, as groups or as individuals, exhibit as a result of (or in response to) some ceremonial celebration—a wedding, funeral, halftime at a football game, High Mass. Most likely the ceremonial occasion involves its participants in a "performance" that goes beyond the confines of music-making; it may be a *Gesamtkunstwerk* of design, costuming, color, pageantry, poetry, dance, food, and drink—and

music as well. During the last few centuries, musical performance has acquired the status of self-sufficient, independent
ceremonial. And when people gather in groups to listen to music, they will behave in culturally approved "ritual" ways which
vary widely according to the style, situation, and society.

Concert-giving and concert-going in Western society can be
used as examples. Prior to attending a typical concert, we likely
have a great deal of information about it: we know the date, the
names of the performing artists, probably the titles of the pieces
they will play, and the price of a ticket (on the further assumption that ability to pay that price is the sole requisite for admission). Once at the concert, we will very likely expect to be seated
in a largish chamber called a hall, with all seats facing toward a
raised platform upon which the performers stand or sit. According to the usual custom, the musicians will not speak to us during the performance; they will not move about (nor will we); we
will not speak to them (or to each other); we will not be eating
or drinking. In fact, it is assumed that we will be intently con-
centrating upon the music as long as it is in progress.

It may appear, to the typical concert-goer, that these customs
have existed since the dawn of recorded history, but in fact none
of them is more than a few hundred years old. They simply
define one particular "ritual" appropriate to a particular kind of
musical occasion. Performers have their rituals, too—situations
in which they may speak to the audience, or to each other, proper
moments for retuning their strings (between movements, but
not otherwise), occasions when pianists may read from the printed
music (chamber performances) and those when they may not
(solo recitals). Ensemble playing usually focuses upon issues of
tight synchronization and interdependence, rather than on individual independence; "teamwork" is especially important in interpreting the standard literature. Traditional Western notation
assigns the performer certain roles and tasks, rather than others:

fidelity to specific instructions regarding pitch and duration; some flexibility with regard to volume, pace, and articulation; the overall task of reading a "language" of written symbols (concerned with all of the above) *while performing*, and at the speed of the music, rather than privately and reflectively. Again, this is not universal practice, but one example of particular ritual behavior.

This century has witnessed a great many attempts to reexamine familiar musical rituals. Composers have asked their performers (or their audiences) to move about, perhaps to speak. Traditional notions of ensemble "teamwork" often dissolve in individualistic, quasi-improvisatory gamesmanship (the difference reflected in new notation as well). Stuffy concert halls are often replaced by more provocative performance spaces— courtyards, factories, moving vehicles, even underwater locations—or by the unique space (and ritual) of loudspeaker/headphone transmission.

Among my own works, I could cite *Elevator Music* (the audience in a moving elevator, the players in vestibules outside the elevator doors) or *Radio Games* (an antiphonal "dialogue" of sorts between players in a radio studio and listeners at home) as extreme instances of this concern. In *Magic Music*, which ostensibly begins as a piano concerto, the grand piano itself (i.e., the physical object) becomes a sort of totem for orchestral performers who gradually gather around it, stroke its strings, rap its wooden case, and shout into its resonating sound-interior . . . in fact, driving the poor pianist away to a nearby organ, where a duet between organ and offstage trumpets eventually comes to dominate the texture. In a number of orchestral works—*Island* and *Eclipse III*, to name just two—I ask players to speak, whisper, cry out, snap their fingers, and otherwise depart from the traditional concert format of performer decorum.

I have also composed many pieces for ensembles that make

use of electronic tape: *Extended Clarinet* (clarinet and tape), *Music for Napoleon and Beethoven* (trumpet, piano, and tape), *Memorabilia* (cello and tape), and others. It has only recently occurred to me that my real fascination with electronic music lay not in the nature of the sounds issuing from the loudspeakers, but in the loudspeakers themselves. The speakers can enlarge the dimensions of "performance" in every one of the ways we have been discussing. By their placement within and around the performance space, they interact acoustically and visually with the architecture; they may attract, divert, or compete for our attention in the context of a larger ensemble; they can set up exciting antiphonal balances throughout the entire performance area. Most interestingly (for me, at least), loudspeakers can be quite commanding as physical objects. With their "magical" powers, they can inspire somewhat the same awe in which pre-literate societies hold their skin drums or bone flutes; the neat geometric shapes of speakers, and their impassive grid faces, can present a marvelously dehumanized, robotlike foil for the living human musicians with whom they interact. In short, the fact that sounds can come out of a little box placed wherever I choose, subject to the laws of gravity, is more relevant to my compositional thinking than any choice of one particular sound or another. *Which* sounds are more appropriate for this or that passage, in this or that work? That would be an entirely different—important, but secondary—matter.

(4) *Illusion*: the inevitable consequence of engaging in an activity with close ties to "magic," mystery, diversion, and storytelling. This fourth (and final) factor enters into every performance and has been hinted at in the last few paragraphs. The special quality of a musical performance rests, in part, on our willingness to "suspend belief" in some aspect of the experience—to delight in assumptions, contradictions, sleight-of-hand trickery, and occasionally even sheer nerve. We enjoy having our senses

teased, our expectations jostled by surprises, and our reflexes tested, often due to a manipulation of the other performance factors mentioned earlier: the space, the assumed ritual, the nature of the sounding bodies.

Here are a few examples of illusion in action. (a) We hear a slow, lyric passage for piano—perhaps one by Chopin—and respond to the pianist's "singing" tone. But the piano doesn't have that kind of tone at all. In fact, every note struck is percussive; a piano melody is made up of many individual sounds going *thunk-thunk-thunk*. (b) We listen to a Bach harpsichord prelude, one with many arpeggiated figures, and imagine that a chord progression is being sustained. But harpsichord tones have virtually no staying power: the illusion of a harmonic "line" is created by the many arpeggiations, just as the illusion of a melodic line will be enhanced by trills, mordents, and other decorations. (c) Singers performing Gregorian chant, in perfect tune and in a properly resonant space (such as a cathedral), can sometimes activate higher overtones. At times, then, a group singing in unison-octave doubling may produce a ghostly resultant fifth; a perfectly tuned performance of organum with octaves and fifths may sound like a succession of triads—shades of Debussy! (d) The very opening of Strauss's *Also Sprach Zarathustra* is not, as laymen mistakenly recall, the famous 2001 horn motif; it is the low, low C of a large organ. That very low note, when heard live in the concert hall, affects listeners in two different and simultaneous ways. First, it is so low that we may not even be conscious of hearing it for a few moments; instead, we may begin to feel a mysterious vibration—perhaps in our chairs, perhaps in the pit of our stomachs. Second, because of the eccentric (and very often concealed) placement of organ keyboards and pipes in concert halls, we may not be able to tell where the note is coming from.

(e) We listen to the "Bourreé" movement of a Bach cello suite, or a Chopin "Mazurka" for piano, and realize that in either case the music has roots in a dance—that is, in a pattern of rhythms, stresses, and pace belonging to the world of social intercourse. We can still recognize references to the stylized physical movements of human beings; here is a spot where there might have been a bow or a curtsy, there a sharp accent where a foot might have been stamped. But the sophisticated abstraction drawn from the dance has been "stylized" in a different direction: undermined by harmonic subtlety that alters the rhythm, or flexibility in tempo, or idiomatic instrumental figuration, or expressive argument, it has become something undanceable. (f) A very rapid running passage in Milton Babbitt's *Ensembles for Synthesizer* sounds as though it were being played on a keyboard of some sort, and for an instant we visualize a pianist with flashing hands executing the phrase in question. But Babbitt's pattern has been punched on a paper roll and fed into an electronic device. It is actually sounding at a tempo faster than that cleanly attainable by any human hands, although our ears don't grasp the implausibility of the situation.

This last example brings us to electronic technology, and (as we might expect) to a host of twentieth-century illusions. One of these was suggested in the preceding example: the image of a human "performer" even when there is none, unless we count Babbitt himself operating the controls of the synthesizer. Many composers, dissatisfied with traditional realization of their ideas by fallible, mercurial human players, have turned to the tape medium as an alternative. They prefer to have their music fixed for all time, as permanent as a work of sculpture. In that sense, the tape or record of Babbitt's *Ensembles for Synthesizer* is not a preserved performance of the piece: it *is* the piece. Paradoxically, though, there are many possible "performances" of an electronic work such as *Ensembles for Synthesizer*, depending upon the nature of playback equipment, the location for listen-

ing, the separation of loudspeakers, one's choice of volume setting—in short, all the traditional variables of space and ritual.

The use of electronics may create other sorts of illusions as
well. Sounds picked up by a microphone, amplified, and fed
through loudspeakers can become pawns in an elaborate game
of space, directionality, distortion, and magnification, as whispered, nearly inaudible "private" sounds are made powerfully
"public." Thanks to the existence of radio, the vast performance
space of a concert hall or cathedral—large enough to accom-
modate dozens, even hundreds, of sounding bodies—can be
shrunk to the dimensions of a little box on our kitchen table, or
a rectangular opening in our automobile dashboard. When we
sit in the car listening to a Beethoven symphony, perhaps imagining that a live orchestra of sixty to eighty musicians is assem-
bled in a concert hall at that moment, playing for our benefit,
we may forget the more likely possibility—that the only immediate "performance" taking place is the engagement of cartridge,
needle, record, and turntable in some tiny, shabby radio studio.
(A badly scratched record heard on the air is especially disturbing to many listeners, not so much because it interrupts the
continuity of sounds, but because it jolts the ears from the illusion of one supposed "performance" to the reality of another.)
The disc containing the sounds of the Beethoven symphony op-
erates within another frame of illusion; the recorded performance we hear is usually not a single continuous realization at
all, but an assemblage of many edited "takes" spliced together
by a studio engineer—in reality, a form of tape composition.

None of this is really new to the world of the arts, of course.
Instruments have traditionally derived their strength and their
charm (perhaps their initial existence as well) from their attempts
to approximate the gestures of other instruments: the violins of
the seventeenth century modeling themselves after operatic
voices, the clarinets and pianos of the Romantic era trying in

their turn to sound like violins, and then the early synthesizers of our own century aping the timbral characteristics of pianos, clarinets, violins, and every other known acoustical instrument. To follow a similar curve in a different medium, consider the theatre of the proscenium stage with its missing "fourth wall," affording us a glimpse of supposed real life; then the early motion pictures, many of which were little more than filmed stage plays; even more recently, the beginnings of television, created on the premises and assumptions of small-screen movies (or visible radio).

As genres or media reach maturity, they inevitably acquire a certain idiomatic confidence. In this regard, a clarinet or stage play or synthesizer can now (if it and/or its creator chooses) simply be *itself*, with its own unique eccentricities, rather than a copy of anything else. Television images are no longer regarded as tiny movies; on the contrary, some audiences may think of the film screen as an enormous TV and the theatre as a giant living room, just as they may regard the live concert-hall performance as a curiously animated variant of a recording. All of these situations simply increase the capacity for "illusion"—especially for a creative artist who wishes to stress that aspect of performance and realize its potential.

I happen to be such a composer, and I have tried to use ambiguity, surprise, and musical sleight of hand as positive factors in much of my own work. In my orchestral pieces *Island*, *Dream Overture*, and *Magic Music*, the live on-stage orchestra is occasionally enveloped by a recorded orchestra emerging from loudspeakers. The performers in my *Areas* (six musicians and six dancers) are asked to exchange roles, so that the flutist and violinist may "dance"—or at least move in stylized, predetermined ways within an assigned space—and dancers may play the cello (or pantomime doing so). In works such as *A Dream of Bells and Beats* and *Music for Audience and Soloist*, members of the

audience become major performers: role confusion and ambiguity at another, perhaps more fundamental level. During *Extended Clarinet* (for clarinet, tape, and open grand piano used
as a resonating soundbox), the soloist suddenly attacks the keyboard and pretends to be a virtuoso pianist. In *Extended Oboe*
the oboe soloist becomes increasingly hostile to the loudspeakers
and eventually mocks them with outraged, quasi-violent gestures. *Mirrors* is scored for piano solo and two-channel tape of
piano material prepared in advance by the soloist. The net effect
here is oddly like that of a work for three pianos merged into a
single gigantic instrument—especially so because of the complex
imitative material, the identical gestures, touch, and technique
in all parts, and the interplay of three voices (crying, screaming,
humming) which are, of course, all the same voice.

My concern with performance in all of its aspects may be
considered extreme. I admit that, over the years, I have increasingly come to regard my work not primarily as the construction
of specific pitches and durations on score paper but, rather, as
the instigation of performances. When I begin to compose a
piece, I must "see" in my imagination the physical setting, the
performing forces, the faces of the players if I know who they
are, and the feel of the instruments *before* I begin to "hear" the
as-yet-unwritten notes. A special treatment of the space or ritual—such as having musicians stationed in the audience, or a
particular lighting effect—may take on a structural importance
for me, very much as a collection of pitches or a characteristic
rhythm might be important for another composer.

I know I am not the only one to have such concerns. When
the Bowdoin College new music festivals were at their height in
the mid-1960s, I was involved in negotiating a commission for
Pauline Oliveros to write a piece for the Aeolian Chamber Players. At first she refused, simply because she had not met any of
the Aeolians; eventually she agreed to write them a new work,

on the condition that they send her a photograph of themselves. She composed *Aeolian Partitions*, in effect, "from" the photo. Along similar lines, the brilliant trombonist Stuart Dempster has expressed reservations about playing new pieces by composers whom he doesn't know personally. He can better immerse himself in the technique, language, and gesture of a new work if the creation represents a person with whom he's shared a meal, or an evening of tape-playing, or an improvisation session.

In my own work, performance considerations dictate the basic direction—the theatrical argument—of a piece. I then superimpose a surface narrative logic of traditional pitch-duration relationships upon that theatrical argument; that is, I "compose" the piece in the usual way on staff paper. But that activity takes place after the entire performance has been predetermined and "seen" in my mind. Only when the spatial, ritual, or theatrical aspects of a piece work for me, *without sound* (that is, as an effective silent film), am I prepared to add the audio "track." It was crucial to the planning of my *Chamber Concerto I* for contrabass that certain idiosyncrasies of the instrument itself—its great bulk, its surprising lyric warmth, the surprising ease with which other instruments overwhelm it—be explored: that is, I had an early image of a bass line buried by an avalanche of ensemble sound. I also wanted to end the work with that situation reversed, with the soloist's line clearly etched and his orchestral "enemies" vanquished. This concept was eventually articulated as a physical dispersal of forces. The ensemble players quietly leave their seats, walk slowly to the back of the stage area, and play whispered taps on various drums and woodblocks. But these details were worked out before a note was placed on staff paper. Similarly the basic ideas of *Chamber Concerto IV* for saxophone involved: (a) the collision and interaction of timbres, bringing the soloist into conflict with a string body and percussion group, but allowing him to mesh with brass and other single-reed players; (b) movement by the soloist on stage during the piece, in a way that confirmed these timbral juxtapositions; and (c) a formal plan that assigned brief, distinctive motives to these timbral subgroups, stated them all in a simultaneous jumble, and then gradually unraveled them. Only when I was sure of these aims did I begin to write clefs, notes, bar lines, and accidentals.

This approach may represent an extreme position, as I have suggested. On the other hand, I believe that *all* composers—not just those who share my concerns—constantly deal with performance in all its aspects. Style is not an issue here: even with the present-day pluralism that admits Milton Babbitt, La Monte Young, Charles Wuorinen, Sun Ra, Marvin Hamlisch, John Cage, Steve Reich, and George Rochberg as equals, one could still argue that everyone's compositional needs and choices are rooted in "performance"—in those inescapable factors noted earlier. I believe that this has always been so, in every age and culture. More to the point, though, it is demonstrably, overwhelmingly the case in the late twentieth century.

Reasons for this situation are not hard to come by. Our new-found awareness of other cultures and performance traditions has been an important factor. The twin stylistic poles of "total control" and "total freedom," and the great range of positions in between, have led to fascinating performance options which are, in turn, further facilitated by electronic circuitry and computer programming. These have all conspired to bring about a uniquely refined awareness of *spaces, sounding bodies, ritual,* and *illusion,* perceived as only a twentieth-century being could perceive them.

A heightened consciousness of performance—with all its options, challenges, and paradoxes—may, then, be one common concern that unites all the factions of this pluralistic musical universe, whether those factions themselves realize it or not.

As for the second major concern that seems to draw these factions together, I think it is less an issue of artistic material or creative choice than a matter of personal character, will, or a certain kind of courage. This may all sound quite Romantic in the grand nineteenth-century sense, and rightly so. For all its dispassionate, clear-eyed Stravinskian objectivity and its understandable disowning of Victorian sentimental schlock, this century is, in one respect, even *more* "Romantic" than the last. I am referring to the composer's state of isolation and his relative alienation from the musical world-at-large of patrons and public(s), a situation that has steadily worsened since the era of Mozart and Beethoven (the first two composers who were forced to confront it fully). This state makes the very choice of a composing career an act of some defiance, and the musical work itself becomes an outer manifestation of unbelievably strong inner drive. The main difference between our cool twentieth century and the passionate nineteenth is that the immediate heirs of Beethoven made their struggles and insecurities the subject of their work; musically speaking, they had no objections to *telling* the world about their conflict-ridden, defiant selves. We think we are telling a different story, but perhaps we are not.

What Beethoven had to contend with, in the wake of the French Revolution and his own physical disability, was severe enough: the breakdown of aristocratic patronage channels; the lessening of the composer's role as household entertainer and the emergence of a very different role as philosopher-mystic-solitary; the growth of a mass middle-class audience with a tendency to splinter into smaller cultish sub-audiences; the twin passions for spectacular virtuosity and simple, homespun, amateur parlor music; the equally schizophrenic craving for exotic novelty, tempered by a newfound delight in history and reverence for the Great Masters. In the years since Beethoven these problems have been compounded by further political revolutions, two world wars, major economic crises, the invention of the radio and the phonograph, displaced artists uprooted and transplanted from one continent to another, and the gradually increasing influence of non-Western thought: that is, a constant stretching, weakening, and regrouping of the social forces that nourish composition.

If we add to this the more recent breakdown in musical *language*—the staggering array of stylistic options that we have labeled "relativism" or "pluralism"—we can understand why the composer's need for a tenacious, internal, self-motivated drive is greater than ever. All composers must find ways of coping with the stylistic multiplicity around them—and not necessarily the ways they learned in conservatory, either. Many composers create their own personas and eclectic languages, drawing from snippets of this or that influence; some strive for a logical consistency, a super-grammatical integrity that (in the face of pluralism) is admirable in its own right, whether one agrees with the chosen path or not. Others have entered the uncharted territory of "performance art," often working along the frontiers of disciplines for which they have not been trained. (I mean that literally: it is not unusual for someone schooled in sculpture to move into tape music, or for a trained composer to explore graphic arts, or for a painter to create dance. In experiencing such art we frequently witness a test of *courage*, the willingness to walk a personal and professional tightrope. Perhaps that courage is best summoned up in some artists when they venture freshly into a new medium.)

My point here is that all creative artists summon a special kind of courage whenever they practice their art. They must assemble a language, a viewpoint, and a technique from the widest assortment of aesthetic positions ever known. They must do this on their own, in the midst of a technological explosion that alters choices even as they are made, and in the face of general public indifference. Perhaps the only difference between the creative artist and the average citizen is that the artist is braver.

To state this all as simply as possible: in the midst of artistic pluralism, one common bond shared by all composers is a concern for performance, brought about by the anthropological and technological revelations of our century. Of these, the most important have been the development of the microphone, record player, and tape recorder. These electrical devices have altered every dimension of our musical perception, changed our musical habits, and brought untold new stresses and challenges to creative artists.

Composers, in their own individual ways, are trying to tell us about it.

Donald B. Kuspit

Collage: The Organizing Principle of Art in the Age of the Relativity of Art

The first part of the task is to define relativity for the purposes of this discussion; the second part is to bring it to bear on collage, conventionally described (if I may fall back on the dictionary) as "an agglomeration of fragments such as matchboxes, bus tickets, playing cards, pasted together and transposed, often with relating lines or color dabs, into an artistic composition of incongruous effect." The dictionary definition concludes with the statement: "It is a type of abstraction."[1] Note the emphasis on the following: agglomeration, fragments, transposition to an abstract plane, and incongruous effect. Collage composition does not cohere, and there is nothing inherent to it. It is the beginning—one might say, the model—for what has come to be called "junk art," being in a sense no more than an accumulation of the detritus of daily life in a composition that can only loosely be called a "synthesis." It implies an easy shift from the material of life to the material of art—the self-evidence of the relationship between the two. Decisions are involved in its creation—from the choice of material to the "composing" of the incongruous effect—but these seem secondary to the expectation of easy crossover between life and art, the easy "translatability" of the one into the other, with only minor artistic adjustments, represented in the dictionary definition by "relating lines or color dabs." However, these relational factors are crucial, for they complete the crossover. On them, as the formal confirmation of transposition, depends the success of the collage—its viability as a "structure" of relationships between fragments of material, and as a demonstration of the reversible relationship (the continuum) between life and art. The gathering together which collage is about becomes abstract and assumes the mantle of art only when token signs of art are added to the mix; i.e., only when it is aestheticized by being "treated" (shall we say "purified"?) with the residue from a convention of art, traces that once signaled a full-fledged act of artistic creation. The artistic fragments refine the life fragments, giving them appeal to a more contemplative level of consciousness than is customary in everyday life, making them safely formal and aesthetically significant. "Laundered," the life fragments have—to use the critical term supposedly indicative of heightened aesthetic awareness—a "crispness" they did not have in life. This crispness is the sign of their autonomy, their new presence, ineffable as well as spontaneously eternal. The life fragments have been raised from a transient to an eternal present as painlessly as possible. The whole process is so patently a mockery of conventional conceptions of art-making—so summary a practice of the theory of art as imitation of nature—that it becomes hard to take collage seriously as art. It brings the whole idea of art into question, or else makes it seem a risky yet superficial venture.

At first glance, then, the collage approach to art—however much it is assumed to give familiar aesthetic results (whether it does or does not quickly becomes a matter of debate)—does not imply the most rigorous sense of art. This is where the idea of relativity becomes relevant; it accounts for that apparent lack of rigor and becomes a means of tracing its implications and finally of justifying it. The collage is only relatively, rather than absolutely, art. The word "only" signals the seeming sense of inadequacy of the collage in comparison to "real" art—the fall from aesthetic grace and decline in general status of art when it becomes all too obviously relative to life, and above all relative in itself, structurally indecisive or uncertain. It is thus no longer clearly autonomous or self-reliant, and when its relative condition is recognized as incurable, it is no longer self-evidently art. The collage seems adrift in a limbo that is neither life nor art, at least by the strictest standards. It seems to have lost its center of gravity, the clarity of its intention as art. It seems to be an agglomeration of literal fragments of life and art—the letter of both, without the spirit of either.

To speak of the relativity of art seems to reduce it to absurdity, to correlate with the methodological absurdity of transposing the important idea of relativity from the realm in which it originated to a realm in which it does not belong and in which it loses importance. To generalize the principle of relativity from physics to art—to exploit it beyond the boundaries of its customary usage—is inevitably to reduce art to pure physicality, for in its scientific usage relativity is descriptive of the workings of physical reality. To use it non-scientifically is to use it prescriptively, and so to misuse and falsify it. Relativity can only falsify what Baudelaire called "artificial existence," the art which is one of the things in what Hannah Arendt calls the "'artificial' world of things" created by work. If, as Arendt says, "the human condition of work is worldliness,"[2] and the world of the work of art is not the same as the material reality that physics investigates, then to reduce art to its physicality—literalness, as it is called by modernism—is to deny its worldliness, and thereby to deny its identity as art. It is also to become estranged from the work that went into the making of art, as well as to disparage that work by characterizing it, presumptuously and prematurely, as merely physical.

But the idea of the relativity of art is not a reductionist strategy. On the contrary, it signals an expanded sense of the possibilities and effectiveness of art—an expanded sense of the meaning of creativity and of art's worldly role. This becomes clear when we recognize that relativity (and collage) presents itself as a solution to an epistemological rather than a physical problem: the problem of *conceiving* art, not simply the problem of receiving or perceiving what is already regarded as art. The latter unavoidably reflects the former, but is logically secondary to it. The philosophical generalization of relativity by Alfred North Whitehead makes its epistemological character self-evident, as does the self-conscious employment of the idea of relativity in psychological and sociological thinking, perhaps most obviously in the works of Jerome Kagan and Karl Mannheim. Here I will use their expanded conception of relativity—increasingly pertinent and analytically precise as it passes from metaphysical to psycho-social and historical meaning—as a scalpel to dissect collage, conceived as the case in point of the relativization of art, i.e., as *the* exemplification of the use and dominance of relativity in modern art. The modern tendency to relativize both the structure and meaning of art self-consciously accelerates with collage. Relativity becomes the determinant of art's immanent structure and worldly consequence—the inescapably central factor in (to use Whitehead's language) the primordial and consequential nature of the work of art. From Cubist collage on, art can never be understood as anything but relative in its nature, and experience of it can never be anything but relative. In Kant's language, from the modern period on, it is a "transcendental illusion" to assume that art can be "complete" or absolute—that it can exist entirely in itself, on its own terms, rather than relative to those which can never be mistaken for art, which resist becoming those of art, and which are ostensibly indifferent to art, i.e., the terms in which life is given.

Whitehead defines the "principle of relativity" as follows: "That the potentiality for being an element in a real concrescence of many entities into one actuality, is the one general metaphysical character attaching to all entities, actual and non-actual; and that every item in its universe is involved in each concrescence. In other words, it belongs to the nature of a 'being' that it is a potential for every 'becoming.'"[3] In the course of spelling out the implications of "the principle of universal relativity," Whitehead remarks that it "directly traverses Aristotle's dictum, '[A substance] is not present in a subject.' On the contrary, according to this principle an actual entity *is* present in other actual entities. In fact, if we allow for degrees of relevance, and for negligible relevance, we must say that every actual entity is present in every other actual entity."[4]

The ontological emphasis is Whitehead's; it amounts to an insistence on the actuality or presence of each entity in every other entity. That actuality is hardly demonstrable, at least on the level of everyday perception. Rather, it influences our expectations. We look for the variety of other entities in any one entity, rather than regarding that one entity as self-same—self-identified. It is identifiable in terms of its synthesis of other entities, each of which remains a possible part of itself. Collage is a demonstration of this process of the many becoming the one, with the one never fully resolved because of the many that continue to impinge upon it. Every entity is potentially relevant to every other entity's existence, is potentially a fragment in every other entity's existence. This is the relativistic message of collage: the keeping in play of the possibility of the entry of the many into the one, the fusion of the many into the one. Concrescence is, in effect, never finished, however much there may be the illusion of completeness. This is the poetry of becoming—the poetry of relativity—and it is what collage is about: the tentativeness of every unity of being because of the persistence of becoming, even when absolute entity-ness seems achieved.

The incongruous effect of the collage is based directly on its incompleteness, on the sense of perpetual becoming that animates it. It is always coming into being; it has never "been," as one can say of the more familiar, "absolute" type of art. It is always insistent yet porous, never resistant and substantive. Its parts always seem to be competing for a place in some unfinished scene, as if to finally give it the necessary accent that makes it complete. Yet nothing in the collage is necessary; each part is forever contending with every other, pushing every other part out of place, until the very idea of a place in an order becomes meaningless. Even the idea of displacement does not focus what is occurring in the collage. What counts is that it remains incompletely constituted, for all the fragments that constitute it. There is always something more that can be added to or taken away from its constitution, as if by some restless will. The collage seems unwilled, and yet it is willful. The collage is a metaphor of universal becoming, becoming that is arbitrary if self-conscious, as much a matter of blind momentum as directed process. For Whitehead, becoming is finally directed by the "desire" of each entity to be itself by becoming more than itself, in a "decisive" way. Indeed, decision is the final step of concrescence for Whitehead. Decision is described in a subjective way as involving positive and negative prehensions, i.e., ap-prehensions of entities that seem relevant and irrelevant to one's becoming. The subject forming itself is not aimlessly adrift on a turbulent sea of becoming, but steers itself through this sea by *deciding* what might or might not be relevant to its being at any given moment of its becoming. Entities prehended positively become parts of the subject's actuality, "ingress"—to use another Whiteheadean term—into its existence, become constitutive of its concreteness.

Collage sums up, as it were, this process of assimilation: the tentativeness of being in the face of its own becoming, the uncertainty or ambiguity of the workings of becoming. Collage, for the first time in art, makes uncertainty a method of creation, apparent indeterminacy a procedure. Entities rejected for inclusion remain associated with the subject that chooses another kind of actuality, as the defining contour or fringe of that actuality. Collage—and we are talking about Cubist collage, as the first truly relativistic and self-conscious use of collage—is very much about these dark fringes, these absences, as well as about the positive presence of positively ap-prehended fragments. The informal fringe and the formal assertion of substance exist side by side in the collage, subtly mingling to generate its energy. This is a material togetherness, not simply a togetherness of signs, as formalist analysis—lately revived in semiotic terms—would have it.[5] That is, it has to do only secondarily with issues of representation and abstraction; primarily, it is about the establishment of a particular kind of artistic, subjective concreteness. The integration of substance and fringe may not give the kind of unity of being that is customarily regarded as grounding the work of art's necessity. It does, however, constitute a concretely becoming artistic subject which has its unity as much in the potentiality of its becoming as in the actuality of its presence.

This point is made clear when one recalls that, in his original definition of relativity, Whitehead remarked that "non-actual" as well as actual entities could be elements in a real concrescence. The "relating lines or color dabs" of the collage—the vestigial use of primary artistic constituents—are such non-actual (abstract) entities, signs of what Whitehead calls "eternal objects." Color is particularly remarked as such an object, as well as geometric form—always implicit in the use, even the most amorphous automatist use, of line. In collage we find abstract elements as material fragments—elements of a code of abstraction that no longer perform the abstractive function but exist as entities in their own right. These fragments of art have equal status with fragments of life in the collage; they are as concrete, for the purposes of becoming, as life. They have no privileged position in the process of artistic becoming, just as the fragments of life (the traditional model of art) do not constitute a privileged source or root of art. There is no clear-cut, single ground of art in the collage: art is no longer either representational (an imitation of nature issuing in an illusion of life) or abstract (a formal construction issuing in a style). It is a creative, subjective choice of elements emblematic of becoming in general. The being of nature and the being of form lose their primacy in the subjective decisions of art, which can move freely between them to achieve its becoming. They unite in a dialectic of ap-prehension which is under subjective control. They are both subsumed in the actuality of the concrete work of art— "worked over" until they become art. The becoming of art is located not in life or style, but in the relativity of relations between them in a particular situation of concrescence. The collage replaces privilege with equivalence, definitions of artistic being with deconstructions of artistic becoming, unity with energy. The field of the work of art reveals itself more as determined by subjective work than as determined by a preconception of art as a certain kind of object, whether life-referencing or self-reflexive.

Let us get more particular, as a way of bringing the subjective character of the relativistic work of art to the fore—as a way of showing how the decisions that constitute the concrescence of a particular work of art are relative. Jerome Kagan, writing about "the need for more relativistic definitions of selected theoretical constructs" in psychology, asserts:

> "Relativistic" refers to a definition in which context and the state of the individual are part of the defining statement. Relativism does not preclude the development of operational definitions, but makes

that task more difficult. Nineteenth-century physics viewed mass as an absolute value; twentieth-century physics made the definition of mass relative to the speed of light. Similarly, some of psychology's popular constructs have to be defined in relation to the state and belief structure of the organism, rather than in terms of an invariant set of external events. Closely related to this need is the suggestion that some of the energy devoted to a search for absolute stimulus characteristics of reinforcement be redirected to a search for the determinants of attention in the individual.[6]

What are the determinants of the artist's attention? Clearly, this question is more to the point of discovering the fundamentally relative situation of the work of art in its modern condition than are questions of subject matter and style—and than are inquiries as to what a truly modern subject matter and a truly modern style would be. There is no absolute definition of modern; "modern" in fact means this absence of or active indifference to absoluteness. No subject matter or style is, once and for all, modern. Only the artist's living attention is modern; only in exercising his powers of ap-prehension is he up to date. By its seeming indifference to the fragments that constitute it—conveyed by the seemingly random way in which those fragments are gathered together—the collage forces us to turn from the fragments to the attention that selected them, the individuality they acquire by being brought together by a particular kind of attention. They themselves, simply by being fragments, exist in attenuated form as stimuli—but never with any absoluteness, only relative to an individual's attention. Why they might be stimulating depends on that attention and individuality. As Kagan says, "If a stimulus is to be regarded as an event to which a subject responds or is likely to respond then it is impossible to describe a stimulus without describing simultaneously the expectancy, and preparation of the organism for that stimulus.

Effective stimuli must be distinct from the person's original ad-
aptation level. Contrast and distinctiveness, which are relative,
are part and parcel of the definition of a stimulus."[7]

For Kagan, this correlates with Whitehead's subjective process
of positive and negative prehension, on the basis of a previously
actualized ap-prehension (categorization) of actuality: "Man re-
acts less to the objective quality of external stimuli than he does
to categorizations of those stimuli." The categorization or belief
structure which is the already existing core of the entity in process of becoming controls, to a great extent, future actualization
or concrescence of the entity. Its subjectivity is already bound by
its beliefs, its categorization of its own actuality and that of the
entities that constitute its world. Such categorical belief gives it
formal closure and seeming unity—a sense of stable identity,
however limited. In collage, implicit belief or pre-existing categories of orientation—unconscious conditions of choice not
necessarily known even to the artist—determines entry into the
field of operations, the field of artistic becoming. The fragments
that find their way into the field are only superficially found by
chance. Chance is a disguise for the uncertain yet highly personal significance they are felt to have. They are fascinating because they are the objects of a belief that only half knows itself,
and so experiences the world in a chance way. The fragments
are experienced as profoundly meaningful, but the meaning
cannot be spelled out completely and never seems to truly surface—which is what leaves the artist free to arrange the fragments as he wishes, in a whimsical or a willful way. This gives
the collage an aura of creative freedom which is crucial to its
sense of liveliness and to the artist's sense of self-determination.
Freedom and chance, the determinate fragments and the indeterminate sense of their relation, become con-fused, making the
fragments even more stimulating than expected.

All of this seems obvious, but there is a tension, the possibility of self-contradiction in the situation that is less obvious but at its center. The significance the artist finds in the fragments involves as much the deconstruction as the objectification of a belief—dissolving as well as acting upon an existing, if implicit, categorization of the world. This destructive dialectic is typical of the difficulty surrounding any attempt to "recover" a subjective sense of significance from an objective world, particularly when the objects of that world are regarded as absolute and the subject is understood to exist relative to them. Under such conditions, the subject always imagines that its consciousness of itself is a false consciousness. Its consciousness of objects is a true consciousness, and however much it may work against that consciousness by dealing with "deteriorated" objects—worn fragments of objects, suggestive of the relative way objects exist as objects—those objects remain intractable enough to obscure or mute the sense of self that arises from resistance to them. The objects, however fragmentary, dominate the subject's sense of itself; and yet the subject's power of belief in the objects has been shaken. Its categorization of the world seems close to collapse, if only because of its unwillingness to trust itself in the face of the objects of the world. They can be defied, if not dismissed, by being spontaneously rather than categorically regarded—by being regarded relativistically, rather than absolutely. This, at the least, frees the self from its own self-centeredness, the sense of a center that it acquires by reason of its belief structure. The belief structure is up for grabs in the relativistic situation of the collage—and the self is inwardly freed from objects, if not externally free of them. Objectivity is no longer a categorical imperative, but can be creatively conceived. A sense of spontaneity emerges which freshens the sense of individuality. This sense of spontaneity arises, in part, from the resistance of the self to its own unconscious categorization of the world, which becomes conscious in the course of being acted upon. And that very act sets the self against itself, which is one of the sources of its revived sense of individuality.

The collage is the scene of this struggle between an objective and subjective sense of worldliness. The subjective tries to defeat its own sense of what is typically objective by seeing all objectivity in relative terms, which at the same time restores its sense of its own primordial becoming. A sense of subjective, "artistic" becoming emerges in the collage, forever obscure or uncertain in its attribution of meaning—its categorization of or beliefs about the world—because it sees any definitive meaning as detrimental to its sense of becoming, as inhibiting of its sense of its own creative, powerful individuality. Yet that individuality refuses to presuppose itself, and it only reluctantly presupposes objects. It conceives of itself entirely in terms of complete openness—what Smithson called an "open limit"—to becoming. It assumes that it is possible to exist on a completely open horizon of ap-prehension, in which no prehension is preordained as positive or negative. It desires to achieve a state in which choice is unnecessary, in which momentum comes not even from one's resistance to one's own choices, but from entirely selfless becoming, from loss in the creative flux of cosmic becoming. This is the impossible ideal: the loss of both subjectivity and objectivity in the ceaseless flow of entities, the loss of even the most elementary sense of the world in a primordial sense of becoming, in which all choices of being are so relative as to be irrelevant, in which all commitments seem superficial in terms of the total flow of things and feelings. In collage, one is ideally totalized by this indeterminate yet insistent flow.

In practice, the collage displays a situation of irreducible tension between a subjectivity eager to identify itself yet incapable of completely doing so, and an objectivity in the process of breaking down—objects in the process of losing their hold on subjects. If, as Kagan says, "contrast" is "an important key to understanding the incentives for human behavior,"[8] then a major incentive for modern artistic behavior is recognition of the contrast between dynamic becoming, overcoming all beliefs about being, and the undertow of a residual sense of being in this becoming. It is about the dynamics of belief—what Nietzsche called the desire for self-overcoming, so as to become freshly concrete. It is about the primal contrast that emerges when relativity invades the scene of being.

The collage, then, epitomizes the state of contrast between categorization of actuality and expectation of becoming—between categorization which determines expectation, and expectation which rebels against categorization by finding fresh stimulation in the world. The collage demonstrates rebellion against determining beliefs in the very act of articulating them through the choice of fragments. More obviously, the collage is a sum of contrasts which never totalize into a single kind of stimulation. Such lack of totalization, of complete objectification of stimuli in a single object, is crucial to the success of the collage. The sense of a restlessly shifting range of stimuli is the essence of the collage—a restlessness reflecting the individuality of the artist's becoming, as embodied in the willfulness of his attention. The unsettled state of the collage is itself emblematic of the will to individual becoming which emerges from the display of fragments. The collage is a relative state of artistic affairs, where relativity indicates the restlessness of individuality in the process of becoming. As such, the collage becomes emblematic of the task of art at least since Baudelaire: the redemption of individuality in mass society, with its standardizations or categorizations—its banalization or de-individualizing of belief. Collage makes poetry with the prosaic fragments of dailiness. The poetry is a matter not just of recognizing the legitimacy of

choosing one's own context of life from the universal dailiness
and thereby in some sense escaping it, but of not getting locked
into or trapped by this context. It is to be regarded as no more
than a means of operating in the dismal dailiness, to be changed
or discarded as soon as it, too, becomes a possessive, standard
routine. Art teaches one to stay ahead of or to transcend dailiness by manipulating it, juggling its variables in endlessly interesting combinations. This implies a certain purposelessness, but
also the playful purposefulness of continuing to become individual, even if the becoming is only pretending in a world that is
"un-becoming" because it is banal—a world that has ceased to
be anything but itself. The essential playfulness of the collage is
a direct acknowledgment of the relativity of individuality in the
world, as well as a way of expanding that world to include it,
and of expanding individuality to include the world. One can
view this ironically, but to do so implies a serious dedication to
irony as the only way of individualizing in a world of standard
categories.

Ironical contrast seems almost a mannerism in Cubist collage
from the start, but it is so relentlessly pursued that it becomes
visionary. Relativity shows itself succinctly in irony, which, however limited and transient—however quickly it becomes a cli-
ché—becomes emblematic of the dialectic between individual
and world, the emergence of each in the other. The limited
becoming of the individual in the world—perhaps limited to his
being relatively artistic, ironically artistic—in the last analysis
turns out to be essential to the becoming of the world, whose
own concrescence is inseparable from its individuation. Collage, relativistic art, implies such inseparability as an ultimate.
It exists against all the forces that would absolutize one kind of
being at the expense of the becoming of all other beings, thereby
destroying the individuality of all kinds of being. This simple
defiance, which is at the heart of relativism in modern art and

in the collage, becomes possible only when one explodes the object of art into theoretically innumerable fragments that never make more than an ironical whole. Those fragments establish an ironical individuality and locate that individuality in an ironical attention to detail that never adds up to a whole. With collage, art becomes a marginal, ironical way of coming into being without fully realizing one's being, preventing it from being mistaken for absolute, objective being, i.e., one which is unassimilable by any other being, one which is free of subjective becoming.

Karl Mannheim offers a further qualification of relativism with his idea of "existential relativity." This idea "is far from implying a relativism under which everybody and nobody is right; what it implies is rather a *relationism* which says that certain (qualitative) truths cannot even be grasped, or formulated, except in the framework of an existential correlation between subject and object."[9] In the course of characterizing "the existential relativity of knowledge," Mannheim remarks that "the situation facing our thinking today appears as follows: various groups are engaged in existential experiments with particular order patterns, none of which has sufficient general validity to encompass *in toto* the whole of present-day reality."[10] From art's point of view this is not the worst state of affairs; it makes for an easier "existential correlation between subject and object," a dialectic which does not have to trouble with validity because it is an experiment in ordering reality, rather than a way of decisively determining it. Such an existential experiment is a way of acknowledging its relativity.

The collage is an "existential experiment with particular order patterns" grounded by the self-conscious belief in the impossibility of ever finding one with general validity. In fact, the desire is *not* to find one, for that would be to interfere with or even to stop the experiment by making it serious. It would be to end the individuality of the experiment—to destroy it as an experiment in individuality. It would be to end its usefulness as the resistance of an individual against the implicitly assumed (if incompletely articulated) general validity of the social order. Relativistic art denies the as-if absoluteness or assumed validity of the daily world of modern society—the daily world of industrial, traditionless society. It asks that world to be true to itself by denying any traditions of art, by accepting the possible industrialization of art—by accepting in art its own restless sense of possibilities, its own sense of becoming. Not that the collage is industrial, except perhaps to the extent that it uses the wastes of industrial society. And not that these do not in themselves add up to to a kind of tradition—a tradition of dailiness. Rather, it asks the modern world to accept its own refusal to grant general validity to any given world—the modern world's sense of the relativity of worlds (masked and simplified by the idea of a plurality of worlds, all "spiritually" equivalent—none superior or more privileged than the other).

This circular relativism completes itself in Mannheim's conception of "perspectivistic" knowledge as the only way of avoiding historicist or nihilistic relativism, in which every point of view is regarded as equally valid. It is not that—in the collage, as everywhere in the modern world—every point of view is equally valid because none is generally valid. Rather, it is that a point of view or perspective must be self-consciously established, to the extent that it not only knows its own nature but can also deconstruct itself. Perspectives are not simply given; they are not stumbled upon and accepted as long-lost relatives. Instead, they must be worked up or, if already given, worked into, made one's own—experienced as emerging from one's own becoming.

There is already an implicit perspective in the seemingly random fragments of the collage. It is not simply the subjective attitude that results from a certain kind of individualizing attention, but an objective perspective implicit in the kind of things that are likely to end up as fragments and to be brought into the collage. The perspective is implicit in the fragments themselves, and individual attention seeks it out, tries to conform to it as well as to manipulate it for ironical (incongruous) effect.

This perspective in the things themselves implies that collage exists not only subjectively but also as a return to what Mannheim calls "the pre-theoretical vis-à-vis." (Mannheim uses the word *Gegenüber*—here translated as "vis-à-vis"—to avoid the word *Gegenstand* or object).[11] This seems to contradict what was implicit earlier, and what seemed at the very core of the relativistic character of the collage: namely, the idea of the impossibility of an unmediated relationship with reality. This relationship would be one of direct intuition rather than of dialectical or existential correlation, and it would seem to deny the very premise of "relationism." Yet, as noted at the beginning, the material fragments that constitute the collage exist in a certain raw state, and they keep sinking back into a pre-theoretical state by reason of the dubious success of their synthesis into a conventionally unified art object. By not fully objectifying as art— by not absolutely *being* art—they present themselves as objects that seem to resist not only art but also any mediation, and thus they present themselves pre-theoretically. This means that the worldly perspective inherent in them can be discovered—that, in not reaching the level of absolute art, they have fallen back into the general world. In failing to achieve an artificial existence, they appear opposite it as clues to the nature of being-in-the-world. They lose their status as physical stimuli and become sedimented meanings of worldliness, artifacts found in a particular excavation at a particular site of the world. The collage becomes simply a way of panning for the golden meanings of the world, an archaeological investigation into a present (if hidden) truth.

More precisely, the collage undermines our ideas about things by refusing to establish them in a systematic relationship, reducing them to the elements of artistic experience. As Mannheim says, systematization is "the first ordering of the 'elements of experience.'"[12] By not subsuming them in this primary order, collage sets them over against us so that they appear unmediated or pre-theoretical, with an inherent perspective of their own. The collage becomes a medium in which real things can be discovered in their objective meaningfulness, as well as one in which artistic things can be invented for the purpose of achieving meaningfulness, i.e., ironical individuality. The duplicity or doubleness of the collage is a direct demonstration of its relativistic character. Self-contradictory, it seems more self-determining or self-created than if it were completely worldly or completely artistic in the conventional, absolutistic sense.

The collage is, then, self-relativizing. When we think of Mannheim's conception of "the self-relativization of thought and knowledge," we realize that he is describing their collage—artistic—character in modern times.[13] The instrument of self-relativization, for Mannheim, is the epoche, "a type of suspension of the validity of a judgment"—in the case of art, the judgment of taste.[14] Taste cannot be brought to bear on the collage, where the consensus of taste no longer determines artistic value. Taste, an eighteenth-century idea that reached a climax of use with this century's conception of modernism, was a short-lived means of establishing an aristocratic mainstream of art within a situation of its increasing democratization, i.e., its increasing openness to life. This openness is partly Romantic in origin—recall Goethe's idea that Romanticism means that no subject matter is alien to art. But, perhaps more crucially, it has to do with the sense of the expanded means of art, with art's eagerness to share in the explosion of technique characteristic of the Industrial Revolution. Taste involves keeping a restraint on technique, insisting that only the traditional media are sure sources of art. Collage destroys the very idea of a medium, of any one "pure" mode of art. With collage, art is nowhere and everywhere; it becomes a freewheeling way of dealing with random material, emblematic of fragmented experience. Modern experience seems fragmented because one never knows what will impinge upon it, what will turn up in it. It is radically open—radically democratic—because it distrusts categorizations of experience as much as it uses them. It discards its belief structure in the very moment of acting on it, initiating a new concrescence—discovering fresh possibilities of experience—in the very moment of acting on the ground of the old one. Subjective being is constantly being overturned by objective becoming, with its unexpected entities presenting themselves for ingression in one's existence. The entities represented by the fragments of the collage, however much they may be familiar and everyday, come to be part of oneself in a new way because one's attitude toward them "artistically" changes.

Mannheim describes self-relativization as "a new form of relativization introduced by the 'unmasking' turn of mind," which is inseparable from "the emergence of a new system of reference."[15] Collage is an unmasking of art and life as they grope toward new systems of self-reference. The fragmentary character of both is revealed, and from the fragments a new revelation emerges—not mechanically, but by way of what Whitehead calls the "creative flux" of the fragments. The establishment of this condition of creative flux—for Whitehead the category of categories, the ultimate category, the final generalization of the principle of relativity—is what collage is about, so that, in the "atomistic competition" between fragments (to use Mannheim's description of competition in democracy), a new sense of systematic possibilities for both life and art might emerge. The unmasking of old systems is necessary to establish the sense of creative flux and the possibility of new systems, new actualizations of meaningful form. This unmasking, as Mannheim says, "does not aim at simply rejecting certain ideas so much as at disintegrating them. . . . To unmask an idea, thus, is not to refute it theoretically, but to destroy its effectiveness."[16]

Collage destroys the effectiveness of the idea that the imitation of nature is the basis of art—the idea that art's highest achievement is not simply to create an illusion of life, but to function as a kind of representation of it. Life can be directly referenced—directly incorporated into art—but not symbolically referenced. Or at least such symbolic referencing or representation of life is no longer the primary task of art, but simply one element in it. Collage also destroys the idea that life is a stable whole, indivisible—or rather, that the division of life will destroy it. Life still exists in fragments which afford new opportunities for experiencing it, new opportunities for finding meanings in it. Art and life become unexpected in the collage, which gives us the opportunity for a creative relationship with both of them. Neither is destroyed by having traditional ideas about it undermined. The disintegration of such traditional ideas which collage represents—for both life and art—does not disintegrate either. On the contrary, in collage what is most essential in both is revealed: their reality as creative fluxes. They have the same root: the relativistic, creative flux of democratic becoming.

What creative flux means in the practice of collage is described by Mannheim: "We understand, looking at things from our perspective, the possibility and necessity of the other perspectives; and no matter what our perspective is, we all experience the controlling 'stubbornness' of the data (*Gegebenheiten*)."[17] The data of life and art—the fragments—indisputably exist, but there is no necessary logic by which they can be ordered. Their "inner necessity" is found in the intention of our own perspective, our own subjective pursuit of meaningful-ness—our own willingness to suspend our customary judg-ments, our categorical understanding of reality, the reality of life and art. The implication of collage, which appears arbitrary and so disturbing, is that it is extraordinarily difficult to suspend the given meanings, the expected forms, the obligatory order, the traditions (whether personal or social) by which we live, and to establish a creatively open horizon. It is a simple enough message, even socially proclaimed—the message of individual openness. But it is rarely acted upon, and it is generally re-garded as a foolish, romantic rebellion against inescapable lim-its. But the stubbornness, the givenness of the data of life and art are not the same as the supposedly logical limits set upon them and used to control them. All such control aims to domi-nate them in the name of a specific perspective, which becomes a cause—to enlist them in the service of a self-styled heroic, universal cause. Returning to the roots of art and life—to cre-ative flux—in the collage, we realize that no perspective is uni-versal or absolute. From the matrix of fragments of both life and art, subjective perspective must be allowed to freely arise, as a dialectical response—a dialectical emergence.

This makes the collage the climactic realization of the ro-mantic principle in art. Mannheim summarizes this principle by quoting Novalis:

> The world must be romanticized. That is the way to its original meaning. Romanticizing means nothing but raising to a higher level of quality. Through that operation the lower self is identified with a higher self, since our soul consists of a series of qualitatively different levels. This operation is still completely unknown. In giv-ing a noble meaning to the vulgar, a mysterious appearance to the commonplace, the dignity of the unknown to the known, the sem-blance of infinity to the finite, I romanticize it.[18]

With collage, relativity becomes *the* way of romanticizing the world, counteracting what Breton calls "miserabilism," "the depreciation of reality in place of its exaltation."[19] By fragmenting the stubborn datum of reality until it becomes a raw stimulus—a fragmentation which encourages relationism and perspectivism to reconstitute reality into an exalted or mysterious semblance of a whole—the collage raises "our soul," as well as the world, "to a higher level of quality." Both come to seem infinitely extensive while bound to an irreducible stubborn fragment of reality.

For Mannheim, there is something fake as well as necessary about this forced march to the depths, this depreciation of the surface to evoke enigma where there may be none. As he says, "the romantic preoccupation with these 'depths' was not a true one. The predominance of the subjective approach introduced an arbitrary element into its interpretations and prevented the thinker from really getting inside his subject."[20] The elusiveness of the collage, its deliberate cultivation of relativity of appearance to undermine the absoluteness of reality—to get behind that façade of absoluteness in order to recover the reality of its becoming, its dialectical metamorphosis in its concretizing of its world—is at once an attempt "to sound the 'depths' of the soul" and "an ideological dressing-up of things as they are."[21] Collage accomplishes both. It evokes the sense of an independent depth of consciousness, of consciousness directed toward itself, clarifying its own perspective; and it evokes the sense of consciousness dressing up "things as they are" with the "profundity" of its own perspective, with the subjectivity of its own interpretation of reality. The seemingly unqualified subjectivity of the perspective counts for more than its regulatory power over reality. In response to Braque's dictum, "I love the rule that rectifies the emotion," Juan Gris said, "I love the emotion that rectifies the rule."[22]

And as one art historian observes, "nowhere did he [Gris] so completely give himself over to his feelings as in his collages, on which he conferred a highly personal magic, interlocking reality and unreality like meshed gears."[23]

The untraditional collage is preferable to the traditional painting because of its greater romantic possibilities, the greater freedom of expression possible in it, and the greater ease with which traditional ideas of what a work of art should be—the realization of a "definitive" style and an imitation of nature—can be dismissed. Relativism is the ideal instrument for romanticization of reality—the flotsam and jetsam of everyday life set adrift in the collage—because it denies certitude of style and nature, of ideals and models for art that might lead to its perfection. Instead of trying to perfect art and to indicate that art is a perfection of life, the collage, in an attempt to "keep alive a certain germ of experience . . . always splits up and relativizes what we believe to be 'rational' and 'objective,'" revealing a hidden "world of 'pure experience.'"[24] The myth of pure experience— immersion in creative flux—sustains collage, not only dismissing traditional ideas of the purpose of art, but also dismissing modernist ideas that the "art" in art has to do with its making. The collage seems casually, even flimsily made, deliberately flawed as a constructed object. It has a ramshackle, helter-skelter look, as though the artist were unsuccessfully trying to clean up an accident. But it is precisely by being poorly made, as it were, that it "breaks into the 'here and now,'" "the first form of utopian consciousness."[25] By being inadequate as an object it acquires "an ecstatic center"[26] beyond its constituents. No longer strictly "congruent with existence"—and so no longer contained by even the thinnest illusion of a circumference, except by reason of its technical termination—the collage seems to center experience in the intensity of its immediacy, heightening our sense of the stubbornness with which it is given and the stubbornness with which we at once assimilate and resist it by means of our relative perspectives on it.

In sum, the collage is an awkward amalgam of three unresolved elements: (1) purely worldly elements, especially such fragments of dailiness as newspapers; (2) purely artistic elements such as line, color, and shape—the typical constituents of form; and (3) mixed or impure elements, or residual images of an imitated nature, ranging from the famous imitation wood grain and chair caning to traces of such domestic objects as clay pipes and such studio props as guitars. Gris' use of the mirror seems to summarize such elements, for it unequivocally demonstrates the illusory character of imitation by making the "imitation" of reality unmistakable. The elements are already "relative" by reason of their displacement from the life-world into the "art world," and by reason of their fragmentary state. Taken together, seen relative to one another, their relativity seems irresistible and fundamental. For all the stubbornness with which they are given, they can never again be regarded as *absolutely* given. They are an experiment in time and space—which shows that the old idea of modern art as an experiment concerned with articulating the fourth dimension has, for all its charming naïveté, a certain truth to it. It is an imprecise but still perceptive way of acknowledging the relativity of concrescence, and of acknowledging modern art as the major exemplification of such relativity.

Notes

1. *Webster's New Collegiate Dictionary,* 2nd ed.
2. Hannah Arendt, *The Human Condition* (Garden City, N.Y.: Doubleday Anchor Books, 1959), p. 9.
3. Alfred North Whitehead, *Process and Reality* (New York: Humanities Press, 1955), p. 33.
4. Ibid., p. 79.

5. See Rosalind Krauss, "Re-presenting Picasso," *Art in America* 68 (December 1980): 90–96.

6. Jerome Kagan, "On the Need for Relativism," in *The Ecology of Human Intelligence*, ed. Liam Hudson (Baltimore: Penguin Books, 1970), pp. 134–35.

7. Ibid., p. 135.

8. Ibid., p. 136.

9. Kurt H. Wolff, ed., *From Karl Mannheim* (New York: Oxford University Press, 1971), p. 226.

10. Ibid., p. 247.

11. Ibid., p. xxii.

12. Ibid., p. xxiii.

13. Ibid., p. xxxi.

14. Ibid., p. xxv.

15. Ibid., p. xxxiii.

16. Ibid.

17. Ibid., p. xxxv.

18. Ibid., p. xliv.

19. André Breton, "Away with Miserabilism!" in *Surrealism and Painting* (New York: Harper and Row, 1972), p. 348.

20. Wolff, ed., *From Mannheim*, p. xlv.

21. Ibid.

22. Herta Wescher, *Collage* (New York: Harry N. Abrams, 1979), p. 29.

23. Ibid.

24. Wolff, ed., *From Mannheim*, p. xlvii.

25. Ibid., p. lxiv.

26. Ibid., p. lxiii.

J. Hillis Miller

The Two Relativisms: Point of View and Indeterminacy in the Novel *Absalom, Absalom!*

By outraged recapitulation evoked . . .
Absalom, Absalom!

"Imitation," "reproduction," "representation," "reference," "relative," "relation"—these are some of the words needed to discuss the topic of mimesis or, more narrowly, of "realism" in the novel. A curious fact about these words and the contradictory concepts they embody is that several of them lead unexpectedly back to the same Latin verb of incongruous principal parts: *fero, ferre, tuli, latum*. The word means "carry" or "bear," but also "relate" in the sense of narrate. The *fer-* in *fero* is the Latin version of the Greek *phor*, as in "metaphor," literally to carry over or take from here to there, to displace. The *fer-* is present in a multitude of English words: transfer (a translation of "metaphor"), confer, infer, and of course refer. To "refer" is to carry something back to its source, as a referential narrative constantly points back to its origin and base in the real world. A self-referential narrative points to itself, carries itself back to itself. Presumably it is in danger of short-circuiting any reference to the real, and so of becoming a sterile mirror of its own activity.

"Relation" has the same etymology. A "relation" is a telling which carries back to itself or carries again what has already been carried over, namely the events that are narrated. A relation is a "report," the latter word once again marked by the *re-* of recurrence. To report is to carry back. All narrative, it seems, is a line of words which goes away from its source but has, as its primary obligation, to return at last whence it came, back to real events.

A "relative" or a "relation," on the other hand, is someone to whom ties of blood or marriage bind me. Those ties relate me, carry me back to him or her, and force me to bear the responsibility of family obligations.

My discussion of *Absalom, Absalom!* will focus on the relationship between relation as storytelling and relation as the network of family and community ties. Faulkner's relation relates the burden of family relationships to the burden of Southern history, as they are relative to the points of view from which they may be related: Miss Rosa's, Mr. Compson's, Sutpen's, Quentin's, Shreve's, and that of the all-encompassing "omniscient" narrator. My own tale turns on the relation among those three forms of relation or of relativity.

The third such word is, then, "relative" in the sense of "contingent." When I use a phrase like "relativism in the arts," I have in mind some way in which something is essentially limited and partial as a result of its dependence on something else, its source or its context. "Relative" forms a pair with "absolute." A "relative" truth is limited by its ties to its source; an "absolute" truth is untied, true in all times and places. Most often when I use the word "relativity," I mean to make some reference to the limitations of human subjectivity. Even "relativity" as a twentieth-century scientific theory, "Einsteinian relativity," the relativity of space and time, is based on a recognition of the limitations of any conceivable human spectator of the cosmos. However armed with instruments he may be, he can only be in one place at one time. Everything he sees and knows is relative to that perspective.

The modern practice of realistic narration, from the seventeenth century on, is, as Ian Watt long ago showed in *The Rise of the Novel*, closely associated with the concept of individual experience. A narration is validated by the testimony of the individual witness or spectator, whether he is the Protestant autobiographer testifying to his own intimate spiritual experience, or the man in the witness box "narrating his experience on oath" (to use George Eliot's figure in *Adam Bede* for the obligation of the realistic novelist), or a man telling the story of his own adventures and validating them by the fact that they have happened to him (as Defoe's Robinson Crusoe does, or as Marlow does in Conrad's *Heart of Darkness*). The emphasis in discussions of realism from Defoe's day to such modern books as Wayne Booth's *Rhetoric of Fiction* on problems of "point of view" and on the question of the "reliability" of the narrator indicates one of the basic paradoxes of realistic fiction: its validity has historically depended on its being the testimony, however fictionally contrived, of some witnessing narrator, someone who has seen the events with his own eyes. Only what is directly experienced is real and therefore capable of being narrated. On the other hand, this means that the truth of a realistic narrative is relative to the subjectivity of that witness, and so always liable to be distorted or partial—as when George Eliot, swearing to tell the truth as she has seen it or as it has reflected itself in her mind, admits that the mirror of her mind is "doubtless defective." That mental mirror has shown things as they appear relative to a certain point of view, not absolutely. If it is relative, how can it claim to be valid as "a faithful representation of commonplace things," as Eliot defines realism, again in *Adam Bede*? Its validity depends on its relativity, but how can it be an adequate representation of reality if it is merely relative?

The title of this essay, "The Two Relativisms," is meant to distinguish between relative as opposed to absolute truth, and an intrinsic relativity within a structure of elements of similar nature (for example, a structure of words). In the latter case the meaning of a given word or phoneme is relative to the surrounding words or phonemes, and those in turn are relative to it, in a perpetual self-sustaining round—though the word "round" is misleading insofar as it sidesteps the tendency of the context in such structures to widen out and become virtually boundless. Where does the verbal context of a given word in *Absalom, Absalom!* stop, except arbitrarily, since the novel is full of allusions to written history, to the Bible, to Greek tragedy, to Shakespeare, and to modern literature?

The first relativism is caught in those binary oppositions necessary to define it. In order to define the "fictional" or the "mimetic" side, the "real" or "factual" side tends to be taken for granted. It is assumed to be unproblematical, to be what everyone already knows, just as Aristotle's definition of metaphor in the *Poetics* presupposes that the notion of literal language is clearly understood and unequivocal. As long as a theorist remains within such binary terminologies, mimesis cannot help but be defined as subsidiary to reality; the concept of reality cannot in principle be interrogated, since it is the ground on which the whole structure of thought in question is built. All those currently fashionable investigations of modern fiction as distinctively characterized by self-reference or by self-reflexivity, by being about their own processes of representation, are necessarily enclosed within the presuppositions of straightforward reference, reference outside to non-linguistic fact. The concept of "self-reference" is the mirror image of the concept of "reference" and is determined by it as its ground. Self-reference is still reference and therefore is still enclosed within the paradigm of the concept of reference. The notion of the self-referential work of art, moreover, far from being a twentieth-century novelty, is an exceedingly traditional kind of aestheticism. It is a version of the notion of the beautiful self-sufficient work of art, referring to itself and to its own beauty, turned in on itself in sterile narcissism. This notion of beauty is present in Mallarmé's Hérodiade before the mirror and in all her antecedents in nineteenth-century and earlier literature. It goes all the way back to one notion of mimesis present in Plato and even then, as in these modern aestheticisms, defined as relative to a mimesis grounded in external fact.

Against this model can be set that other "structural" form of relativism I have defined. No structure of words—for example, the text of *Absalom, Absalom!*—can be wholly determinate or unequivocal in meaning. The reasons for this are intrinsic to the nature of words as such. My interest is in the *interference* of this second form of "relativism" (the indeterminacy of meaning in works of literature taken in themselves) in the workings of the other form of relativism (the relativism of point of view in relation to a presupposed objective reality). It is not that words are not referential; there is always a referential dimension to any fictional integument of words. Rather, criticism focusing on a novel's "realism" must avoid prematurely short-circuiting the problem of meaning in that novel by placing the act of reference in the wrong place and then using that presumed reference illicitly to solve problems of interpretation. Oral storytelling, and the writing and reading of novels, are perfectly real acts in the real world. They are acts, however, which depend for their existence on a momentary detachment from immediate engagement in straightforward action or speech. When I read a novel I remain in the pragmatic world, sitting in my armchair. But in another sense I have used the book in my hands as a means of detaching myself, at least for a time, from the room, from the chair, from my responsibilities, from all my immediate circum-ambient placing. I use the book as a means of entering another place, the fictional world of the novel, Faulkner's Yoknapataw-pha County, Mississippi, or his idea of a Harvard dormitory on a frigid winter midnight. Novels depend for their existence on the ability of words to deviate from immediate relation to reality and to go on functioning, at least momentarily, separate from that relation—like a locomotive without a driver, speeding on down the tracks.

The nature of such detached collocations of words must be interrogated with care before the mode of their insertion into the real world can be certainly identified. Since *Absalom, Absalom!* is a novel about the function of storytelling in human life, as well as an example of it, it is especially appropriate for a case study of the problems of "relativism" in their connection with the topic of mimesis.

In *Absalom, Absalom!* all the art of modern realist fiction is recapitulated, and all the problems inherent in an attempt to ground the interpretation of fiction on its need to be "realistic" are splendidly exemplified. Forced by exigencies of space to be brief where a virtually interminable commentary would be necessary for anything like an exhaustive following through, I limit myself to a partial exegesis of a single passage, one of a number of such passages in the novel. In them the narrator or one of the characters offers the reader an image whereby he is invited to think of the novel as a totalizing activity which involves fitting many parts together to make a coherent unity. The peculiarity of these passages is quadruple.

First peculiarity: They interrupt the forward linear flow of the narrative as the telling of a realistic sequence of events corresponding point for point, within the fiction, to events that are presumed in fact to have happened. These passages interrupt the narration by presenting a spatial image for those events taken as a whole. The figure may be made of something actually there on the first level of the realistic narration (such as those tombstones in the woods of the Sutpen family that Quentin comes upon with his father), or they may be imposed from the outside as a "like" or "as" by one or another of the narrators. Such figures invite the reader to think of the temporal line as turning back on itself and becoming an emblem, a design of the whole which stands for the meaning of the whole. The straight line of realistic reporting taking the reader from beginning to end of a causally connected sequence of events becomes instead a parabolic curve. The reported events become a parable for something other than the presumed real events of which they are the mimesis. This interference in realism by parable is a normal feature of realistic narrative and is in no way incompatible with realism as such. The parables of Jesus in the New Testament, for example, combine homely realism in narrative with "symbolic" meaning. Both *Wuthering Heights* and *Middlemarch*, to give two very different examples from Victorian fiction, contain such emblematic passages: "These things are a parable," says George Eliot in the well-known passage about the pier-glass. In parable, realistic narration is twisted away from its function as event-by-event mimesis and is made the hieroglyph of something else, some meaning which can be expressed in no other way, as Jesus can give the multitude news of the Kingdom of Heaven only through the enigmatic medium of parable.

Second peculiarity: The emblematic passages which are such a regular feature of realistic fiction, making it a secular version of scriptural parable, tend to concern the activity of narration itself. They are places where the story turns back on itself to speak of its own nature and function. Likewise, commentators have often noted that the parables of Jesus tend to be obliquely *about* parable; they are about the problems of disseminating word of the Kingdom of Heaven through parabolic teaching to those who have eyes but see not, and ears but neither hear nor understand.

Third peculiarity: The various spatializing models presented by the parabolic interruptions in a novel like *Absalom, Absa-*

lom! or *Middlemarch* are all incompatible with one another.
Each stands for the whole story in its relation to some enigmatic
"it" for which the whole story stands, but the inadequacy of
each (or its only relative adequacy) is indicated by the fact that
the novelist needs so many of them and that none is quite congruent with the others. There is a superabundance of them, as if
the novelist were trying, unsuccessfully, various ways of "getting
it right." He throws the figures out into the void, one after the
other—but none of his totalizing formulations seems to work,
since another is always needed and each new one contradicts
the previous ones. If the reader already grasps the "it" which lies
behind the story, then such passages are clear enough: "Whosoever hath, to him shall be given, and he shall have more abun-
dance." If the reader does not grasp the "it," if he is one of those
who "has not," such passages add a further enigma to what is
already enigmatic enough. They take away even such understanding as he has: "But whosoever hath not, from him shall be
taken away even that he hath" (Matthew 13:12).

Fourth peculiarity: All these passages (in *Absalom, Absalom!*
at least) parabolically express the failure of realistic mimesis.
They express the inability to get the story to come out right, the
failure either to understand it and so to have done with it and
free oneself from it, or, on the other hand, to understand it and
so to take possession of its meaning as one's heritage, one's fa-
milial and historical birthright. Such passages express the impossibility either of finishing the story or of continuing it in
one's own life except as the repetition, once again, of the failure
to make it come out right.

One of the many such passages in *Absalom, Absalom!* is spoken by Mr. Compson. He tells the story to Quentin as they sit
on the Compsons' porch in the Mississippi summer, in the min-
gled smell of wisteria and cigar smoke, waiting for it to be time
for Quentin to go out to Sutpen's Hundred with Miss Rosa:

It's just incredible. It just does not explain. Or perhaps that's it:
they dont explain and we are not supposed to know. We have a few
old mouth-to-mouth tales; we exhume from old trunks and boxes
and drawers letters without salutation or signature, in which men
and women who once lived and breathed are now merely initials or
nicknames out of some now incomprehensible affection which
sound to us like Sanskrit or Choctaw; we see dimly people, the
people in whose living blood and seed we ourselves lay dormant
and waiting, in this shadowy attenuation of time possessing now
heroic proportions, performing their acts of simple passion and simple violence, impervious to time and inexplicable—Yes, Judith,
Bon, Henry, Sutpen: all of them. They are there, yet something is
missing; they are like a chemical formula exhumed along with the
letters from that forgotten chest, carefully, the paper old and faded
and falling to pieces, the writing faded, almost indecipherable, yet
meaningful, familiar in shape and sense, the name and presence of
volatile and sentient forces; you bring them together in the proportions called for, but nothing happens; you re-read, tedious and intent, poring, making sure that you have forgotten nothing, made no
miscalculation; you bring them together again and again nothing
happens: just the words, the symbols, the shapes themselves, shadowy inscrutable and serene, against that turgid background of a hor-
rible and bloody mischancing of human affairs.[1]

This splendidly eloquent passage gives the reader not only figures for the experience of all the various narrators inside the
novel, including the encompassing omniscient narrator, but
also an image for the effort (in life or in history, rather than in
narration) of various characters, most notably Thomas Sutpen,
to fulfill a "design," to make something whole—an estate, a
family, a place in the world—which will compensate for the
past. The passage, finally, offers an image for the reader's activity as he goes over and over the text of Absalom, Absalom!,
moving back and forth across the surface of each page, "rereading, tedious and intent, poring," trying to make sense of it,
so he can understand and perhaps forget it. The image of the

chemical formula is a brilliant figure for the attempt in all these areas to make a linear series of dispersed elements become a simultaneous whole.

All these efforts fail. The failure of each is analogous to the failures of the others, a figure for them. *Absalom, Absalom!* is a novel about the failure of narration, the failure of human intentions in history, and the failure of reading to lead to clear understanding. The reader, understandably, wants to know why this is so. Why can he not, on principle, understand *Absalom, Absalom!*? Why is it like a chemical formula that does not work? This desire can be expressed figuratively in a series of analogous questions: Why did the South lose the war? Why did Thomas Sutpen's project fail? Why does Quentin Compson hate the South, and why did he (in another novel, *The Sound and the Fury*, whose relation to this one is by no means unproblematic) commit suicide? Why do none of the narrators in *Absalom, Absalom!* accomplish what they want to accomplish through the act of narration? Why did Faulkner fail as a novelist, and why, in a well-known statement putting down Ernest Hemingway and praising Thomas Wolfe, did he prize most of all those writers whose design, like Thomas Sutpen's and like his own, is so grandiose that it is bound to fail?[2] No reader of *Absalom, Absalom!* can doubt that it is such an ambitious work. It is one of those all-inclusive, roughhewn, hyperbolic giants, a regular Sutpen's Hundred of a novel. Such works are characteristic of American literature. Each is in one way or another unfinished and unfinishable. They lack finish. One thinks of *Moby-Dick* and *Leaves of Grass*, or of the notebooks of Emerson, or of Pound's *Cantos*, of *Look Homeward, Angel* and of *The Naked and the Dead*, even of "The Man with the Blue Guitar" or *Paterson*. Each of these could not, in principle, accomplish what it sets out to do. Its success is in its failure. In the case of *Absalom, Absalom!* this failure is present in the way something is always missing in the effort of living, of telling, and of reading. The author, the narrators, the man or the culture with a design, the reader of the novel are each always left, after the most energetic efforts, with inert ingredients which have not coalesced.

What is the cause of all these analogous disasters, and what is the ground for the analogies among them? The question might be asked in Thomas Sutpen's words: "You see, I had a design in my mind. Whether it was a good or a bad design is beside the point; the question is, Where did I make the mistake in it, what did I do or misdo in it, whom or what injure by it to the extent which this would indicate. I had a design" (p. 263). Many different designs may be distinguished in *Absalom, Absalom!* All are "realistic" in the sense that they want to touch and affect the real, to be adequate to it. The model for all is the pseudo-performative of God's *Fiat lux* in Genesis. God's *Fiat* is a pseudo-performative because it is posited on God's prior knowledge and because it creates the conditions of knowledge and light—the conditions within which things may be seen and known. It is, like all the performatives in *Absalom, Absalom!* itself, contaminated by being or by wanting to be constative, the adequate representation in words of a reality already, in one way or another, there. In the novel Thomas Sutpen's creation of Sutpen's Hundred and his attempt to cut himself off from his actual family and historical roots, so becoming his own instantaneous progenitor, are explicitly compared to God's *Fiat*: "Then in the long unamaze Quentin seemed to watch them overrun suddenly the hundred square miles of tranquil and astonished earth and drag house and formal gardens violently out of the soundless Nothing and clap them down like cards upon a table beneath the up-palm immobile and pontific, creating the Sutpen's Hundred, the *Be Sutpen's Hundred* like the oldentime *Be Light*" (pp. 8–9).

To God and Thomas Sutpen as performative/constative creators by means of the word may be added the attempts to accom-

plish something through storytelling by all the narrators within
the novel, from Miss Rosa ("*she wants it told*" [p. 10]), to Mr.
Compson, to Sutpen himself ("He was telling a story. He was
not bragging about something he had done; he was just telling a
story about something a man named Thomas Sutpen had experienced" [p. 247]), to Quentin and Shreve ("It was Shreve speaking, though save for the slight difference which the intervening
degrees of latitude had inculcated in them [differences not in
tone or pitch but of turns of phrase and usage of words], it might
have been either of them and was in a sense both: both thinking
as one, the voice which happened to be speaking the thought
only the thinking become audible, vocal; the two of them creating between them, out of the rag-tag and bob-ends of old tales
and talking, people who perhaps had never existed at all anywhere, who, shadows, were shadows not of flesh and blood
which had lived and died but shadows in turn of what were [to
one of them at least, to Shreve] shades too, quiet as the visible
murmur of their vaporizing breath" [p. 303]), and finally to any
reader or critic of the novel who becomes in his or her turn the
recipient of the words and is forced in one way or another to
evoke again these shadows, to tell the story again, to relive it, to
become himself or herself these characters and to repeat their
lives, as Shreve and Quentin do when they become Charles
Bon and Henry Sutpen riding toward that moment when Henry
will turn his horse and shoot Charles "dead as a beef" (p. 133).[3]

The motivations of each of the narrators can be analyzed in
detail, distinguished, and specified, but for all it is in one way
or another the case that the demand of narration made upon
them is double. On the one hand, they want to understand the
past, to make sense of it through retelling it, by sorting out the
facts, ordering them, and interpreting them. They want to free
themselves from the past by gaining knowledge of it through
saying it over; for example, Thomas Sutpen goes patiently over

the facts of his own life, trying to figure out where he made the mistake that caused his design to fail. On the other hand, all these narrators want to use the performative power of evocation in storytelling to make something happen now. They want to take revenge on the ghosts of the past, to free themselves from those ghosts or to pass them on to other people. They all want in some way or another to use words as a form of action.

The simplest explanation for the failure of all these efforts of narration would be to say that the performative and constative functions of language are incompatible and contradictory. Each inhibits or thwarts the other. They cannot be accomplished at once, yet no storytelling can choose between them. No storytelling can be one mode alone. It cannot purify itself of contamination by the other mode and be all constative or all performative. The necessary failure of narration lies in this failure, which is dramatized in *Absalom, Absalom!* in terms of the opposition between miscegenation and incest. This opposition is voiced explicitly in that confrontation between Henry and Charles Bon in the cold dawn when they are on bivouac during the seemingly endless Southern retreat. This is the encounter in which Henry warns Bon that he will kill him if he tries to marry his sister. Bon answers: "So it's the miscegenation, not the incest, which you cant bear" (p. 356).

As anthropologists have demonstrated (for example, Sir Edmund Leach in a well-known essay on the genealogies of the Old Testament[4]) the problem in a closed community such as an Israelite tribe in early Old Testament times is to avoid in the marriages which carry on the tribe from generation to generation either too much sameness, in one direction, or too much difference, in the other. Too much sameness is incest, the same mating with the same. Incest is a pollution of the bloodline through an excess of purification. The narcissistic perversity of incestuous desire is brilliantly dramatized in Henry's love for his

sister Judith in *Absalom, Absalom!* She is his other self, his mirror image. He desires to possess her through Charles Bon's possession of her, and even thereby to be indirectly possessed by
Bon. His love for the latter is like that of a woman for a man.

Too much difference is miscegenation, the same mating with
the wholly different, introducing so much difference into the
community that the bloodline is hopelessly contaminated, the
community in danger of ceasing to be itself. As Faulkner's *Absalom, Absalom!* shows, in part through its explicit echoes of an
Old Testament story of incest and intrafamilial warfare,[5] the
white slave-owning plantation families of the antebellum South
were as much caught between these contradictory taboos as was
any "primitive" tribe. If too much sameness is bad, too much
difference is even worse. As *Absalom, Absalom!* indicates, the
violence of the taboo against miscegenation is even more com-
pelling, more absolute and finely drawn, than the taboo against
incest. An eighth, a sixteenth, a thirty-secondth, even the tiniest
soupçon of black blood makes someone a forbidden partner for
lawful marriage intended to produce children who can be as-
similated into the white community.

The story of Charles Bon's son by his octoroon mistress, Charles
Etienne de Saint Velery Bon, a story anticipating that of Joe
Christmas in *Light in August* and interwoven as a kind of sub-
plot into the main story of *Absalom, Absalom!*, shows what it
means to say that the double prohibition is an impossible contradictory taboo. Charles de Saint Velery Bon can neither be
black nor white. He is torn to pieces by that impossibility, rejected by both the black and the white communities, savagely
and repeatedly beaten by both blacks and whites, unaccepted by
either race. He is a man without a race, without a community,
without an identity—a true pariah.

It is the miscegenation, not the incest, which neither Henry
nor his father can bear. Henry will accept the incest but he can-

not tolerate the fact that, as Bon puts it, "I'm the nigger that's going to sleep with your sister. Unless you stop me, Henry" (p. 358). Thomas Sutpen cannot allow himself to make the least gesture of recognition toward Bon or in any way to accept him as his son. To do so would be to destroy in an instant his design of the foundation of an immaculate dynasty to compensate for the snub he received as a boy when he was turned away, poor white here the mirror image of black slave, from the plantation door. Far from achieving that compensation, he is destined simply to repeat what happened to him at the beginning, turning his own son away as he himself had been rejected, and dying with no male heir but Jim Bond, more black than white, to carry on his line.

Sutpen can achieve that compensation only by cutting himself off wholly from his past and creating by something like the divine *Fiat* a clear design, pure and self-generated, a design made of nothing but his own will and boundless masculine power: "Be Sutpen's Hundred." There must be no otherness and no debt to others. Sutpen wants to be beholden to no man or woman. He must not imagine himself as in any way indebted to them or obligated to them. His design is analogous to the inturned narcissism of incestuous desire. This fact is externalized in the destructive triangle of incestuous brother-sister and brother-brother love in his three children: Henry loving Judith and seducing her through Bon, Bon seducing Henry rather than Judith, Judith loving Henry through Bon. Nevertheless, Sutpen needs other people for his design. Any otherness is too much, but he must have other people and objects—land, a house, possessions—to shape to the pattern he has in mind, though he wants them to be purely "adjunctive" or "incremental." "I had a design," he says. "To accomplish it I should require money, a house, a plantation, slaves, a family—incidentally of course, a wife. I set out to acquire these, asking no favor of any man"

(p. 263). Of his rejection of his first wife and her child, Charles Bon, when he finds she has black blood, he says: "I found that she was not and could never be, through no fault of her own, adjunctive or incremental to the design which I had in mind, so I provided for her and put her aside" (p. 240). But of course he can never put her aside. His unconquerable innocence lies in thinking he can do so. In relating himself to her he has incurred an infinite debt which, like that in all intimate human relationships, can never be paid off.

Unless, that is, the debt is cancelled by "overpassing" to love, as Shreve and Quentin do in their extraordinary collective narration, that evocation in which they become one another and become simultaneously both Henry Sutpen and Charles Bon riding toward the moment when Henry will turn his horse and shoot Charles dead. Overpassing to love, giving himself to another in love, or recognizing the loved person as having a separate existence and value is just what Thomas Sutpen is unable or unwilling to do. As a result, by an implacable law of Faulkner's moral universe, both his design and the man himself are destroyed. On the other hand, those who are able to love, to give themselves to another, as Shreve and Quentin each gives himself to his companion in narration, or as Henry Sutpen is abjectly subservient to Charles Bon, are by no means guaranteed happiness in Faulkner's world. Quite the reverse: they suffer as much or more, and by an equally implacable law. Though it may be better to love, whether you love or not you will, for Faulkner, regret either, or both, and suffer for your choice or for your fate as one who cannot love or who must love.

The effects of the prohibition against miscegenation as exemplified in the results of Sutpen's transgressions of that taboo are only the overt social, economic, and racial versions, appropriate for the specific conditions of the pre–Civil War South, of the more general law that another person cannot with impunity be made into an impersonal element in a subjective design. Sutpen's immorality is the immorality of slavery, which treats persons (a black woman, for example, used to satisfy a young plantation owner's lust) as objects. Southern male chauvinism, which puts women on pedestals, as they say, so subtly degrading them into symbols of sexual purity, is the mirror image of the institution of slavery in the antebellum South, as many social historians have noted, and as Faulkner shows brilliantly. Sutpen's way of treating Ellen or Rosa or Milly, or even his daughter Judith, is no different from his way of treating his first wife or the slave mother of Clytie. All are treated as mares to be bred to him as stallion— or, in the case of Judith, to be bred only to a white male worthy to carry on his line on the female side. What he fails to recognize, perhaps even as the scythe wielded by Milly's grandfather, Wash Jones, descends to kill him, is that his relation to each of these women incurs an infinite obligation. He can never balance the moral ledger once he has allowed any otherness at all into his design, whether that is the otherness of another race in miscegenation or merely the otherness of the other sex in his need, "incidentally of course," for a wife in order to found a family. The calculation never comes out right; the ledger can never be cleared. There is always "one nigger Sutpen left" (p. 378) to destroy the purity of the design. As a result the story is condemned to repeat itself once more, with a similar unsatisfactory result, as Charles Bon reenacts in a different way his father's life, or as Henry does, or as Charles Etienne de Saint Velery Bon repeats his father's and grandfather's, and Jim Bond presumably repeats that of the whole line, and so on, until the Jim Bonds "conquer the western hemisphere" (p. 378), fulfilling Quentin's affirmation that "not only a man never outlives his father but not even his friends and acquaintances do" (p. 277).

   The failures of narration are analogous to the failures of actual designs in life. This connection between moral design and

narrative design is made explicit in a crucial passage in which
the narrator comments on the collective evocation of the past by
Quentin and Shreve:

> That was why it did not matter to either of them which one did
> the talking, since it was not the talking alone which did it, per-
> formed and accomplished the overpassing, but some happy mar-
> riage of speaking and hearing wherein each before the demand, the
> requirement, forgave condoned and forgot the faulting of the
> other—faultings both in the creating of this shade whom they dis-
> cussed (rather, existed in) and in the hearing and sifting and dis-
> carding the false and conserving what seemed true, or fit the
> preconceived—in order to overpass to love, where there might be
> paradox and inconsistency but nothing fault nor false. [p. 316]

Storytelling is, as this passage says, in response to a "demand."
It is a "requirement." This demand is as imperious and as impossible to fulfill as the demand to love or not to love, whether
the demand for narration is made on Rosa, who "wants it told,"
or on Sutpen, who must tell it over to figure out where he went
wrong, or on Quentin, who must tell it over again in order to
try to come to terms with his Southern heritage, or on Faulkner
himself, certainly a novelist whose writing responds to some obscure demand for storytelling.

The analogy between the failure of a design in life and the
failure of narration may be expressed as a ratio: incest is to performative narration as miscegenation is to constative narration.
If Thomas Sutpen and his children are caught between incest and
miscegenation, between the desire to be entirely self-sufficient
and the taboo against that, on the one hand, and the need to
appropriate the unlike and the taboo against that, on the other,
narration is undone by the impossibility of being either purely
performative or purely constative.

If a storyteller tries to stick to the external facts and to reflect them in a perfect mimesis giving valid knowledge, evoking the past exactly as it was, sooner or later he starts extrapolating from the known facts and inventing episodes that may or may not have happened—as Shreve and Quentin do in their retelling of the story of Henry's murder of Charles. They do this perhaps, as Faulkner's narrator says, in order to "perform" and "accomplish" the overpassing to love, but in doing so they "discard the false and conserve what seemed true, or fit the preconceived." That is, they alter the facts as known or go beyond them, beyond mimesis, to create something which is in one degree or another a fiction not wholly grounded in its exact correspondence to things as they are. Like all the other narrators in the linked chain of storytellers in *Absalom, Absalom!* they do this in order to make their story "perform," do something, accomplish some purpose in relation to themselves or others. They try to use story-telling to make something happen in the world. In adding to the facts, however, they fail to fulfill the demand for a wholly accurate narration. What they "evoke" has no grounds but their performative, evocative voices. What they evoke may be "people who perhaps had never existed at all anywhere"—as Henry, Bon, Sutpen, and the rest in fact did not. The performative "faults" incur an obligation, another demand for narration; so the story must be told again, and again, and yet again, without hope of ever getting the story exactly right and so never having to tell it again. The demand for narration, too, is a debt which can never be paid off, just as the use of other people to ac-complish a private design incurs a debt which always ruins the design. "*I am going to have to hear it all over again*," thinks Quentin, "*I am already hearing it all over again I am listening to it all over again I shall have to never listen to anything else but this again forever*" (p. 277).

In the other direction, the temptation of incest is parallel to the temptation of an effort of narration which wants to assimi-

late the recalcitrant particularity of human life and history to a
grand, coherent fictional design. It wants to dominate life by
turning it into words, to internalize life in a fiction, to aestheticize it in a perfectly self-contained, self-reflexive work of art.
This is the temptation to sever art from life and to make it a self-
sufficient performative realm ungrounded in anything but its
own activity. The sign of this motive for narration is the desire
to present the temporally sequential all at once, so it can be
grasped as a simultaneous spatial design. Thomas Sutpen tries
by a tremendous effort of will to hold Sutpen's Hundred together as an accomplished design, *as though in a prolonged
and unbroken instant of tremendous effort embracing and hold-
ing intact that ten-mile square while he faced from the brink of
disaster, invincible and unafraid, what he must have known
would be the final defeat*" (p. 163). "Be *Absalom, Absalom!*" in
this, too, is analogous to "Be Sutpen's Hundred." The mode of
this form of narration is the parabolic emblem, those moments
when the forward-flowing stream of storytelling turns back on
itself to try to gather all of itself in a single image.

   This form of narration fails no less than the other—as does
Sutpen's attempt, for all who engage in it, though for an opposite reason from the failure of constative narration. It fails
because no performative use of language can be purely performative; it is always to some degree inhabited by constative reference. If in one direction a storyteller tries to stick to the facts
(the constative effort), and ends by inventing them (the performative element), in the other direction if a storyteller tries to
invent a purely fictional story, wholly cut off from life, if he tries
to absorb life into a perfect narrative design, he always ends by
referring to life and to history, since the words he must use are
after all referential. It is not so much that writers or critics can
successfully commit the sin of putting the referential, mimetic
aspect of language in brackets, as some writers and critics are

accused of doing. It is, rather, that all writers and critics are
doomed despite themselves to name the real world. We are all
condemned to reference, though that may be our salvation. All
writers necessarily bring the recalcitrant, contradictory, inconsistent quality of life and history into even the most formally perfect story.

The evidence for this in *Absalom, Absalom!* lies in the way
all those emblematic images which punctuate the novel express
incompletion and dissatisfaction. They show how all attempts at
wholly coherent storytelling are undermined by an "it" which
makes the story fail to come out right. The storyteller puts all
the ingredients of the chemical formula together, and nothing
happens. The recipe does not make pie or cake as it is supposed
to do. There is always one nigger Sutpen left over. The ledger
cannot be balanced, cleared, its pages torn out and burned. The
effort must always begin again in an always unsuccessful attempt
to make the story self-contained and consistent. This failure of a
narration is, for Faulkner, the evidence of its validity, since only
the failed narration, which exposes its loose ends and inconsistencies, can be an adequate representation, figure for what has
no literal name, of that unnameable "it." This "it," for Faulkner, undermines both human life and human history in one
direction and storytelling in the other. It is in failing that life
and art ultimately correspond. Art is mimetic after all, by not
succeeding in being otherwise. The story's failure as coherent
design is necessary to the accomplishment of Faulkner's ultimate
design, which is to give knowledge, however indirect and fleeting, not of the facts of history or of life, but of the enigmatic
power behind these. That power is named in the image Shreve
proposes of the "Creditor" to whom Thomas Sutpen, as Faust,
has an infinite debt, and who will eventually call in the debt
and destroy him (pp. 178ff.).

Far from constituting the solid ground that the critic seeks for the interpretation of narrative, the topic of mimesis has led once more to an encounter with the obscurity of the fact that all narrative is a figure for something which cannot be adequately figured, much less adequately named in straightforward referential language. For Faulkner in *Absalom, Absalom!*, living and storytelling are inextricably intertwined. To live is to narrate, because to live is to relive, and to narrate always to renarrate, to tell it over again. No man or woman can not live, not narrate, as long as he or she breathes. It is an absolute demand, a demand which can never adequately be met. It therefore always has to be responded to again as it is passed from person to person, as that letter from Charles Bon, written in frail, spidery script, is transmitted as legacy from reader to reader evoking the dead. The critic, too, you or I, encounters once more this demand when, motivated by whatever necessity or chance, he or she picks up a copy of *Absalom, Absalom!* and begins to read.

Notes

1. William Faulkner, *Absalom, Absalom!* (New York: Vintage Books, 1972), pp. 100–101. Further references to this edition will be noted by page numbers in the text.
2. See *Lion in the Garden: Interviews with William Faulkner* (New York: Random House, 1968), p. 58: "Thomas Wolfe—he had much courage, wrote as if he didn't have long to live. . . . Hemingway—he has no courage, has never climbed out on a limb."
3. My appropriation from J. L. Austin of the opposition between constative and performative language is not unproblematic. The issue remains controversial. Austin himself resolutely excluded literature from the class of true performatives and included it with jokes as an example of an "etiolated" or not serious performative: "I must not be joking, for example, nor writing a poem" (*How to Do Things with Words* [Oxford: Oxford University Press, 1980], p. 9). On the other hand, it is difficult for me to see how literature can, by Austin's own definition ("the issuing of the utterance

is the performing of an action" [ibid., p. 6]), be refused admission as one special class among the wide variety of performatives. To utter a performative: "I bet you can't do it." By the way, if it be objected that God's *Fiat* is grammatically an imperative, it must be said to be an exceedingly peculiar one, since it is not addressed to anyone or to anything, except to the prior knowledge of the possibility of light existing within the mind of the utterer of the command. For this reason I call it a pseudo-performative.

4. The essay is included in Michael Lane, ed., *Structuralism: A Reader* (London: Jonathan Cape, 1970).

5. For the best discussion of the complexities of these echoes, see Stephen M. Rose, "Faulkner's *Absalom, Absalom!* and the David Story: A Speculative Contemplation," in *The David Myth in Western Literature*, ed. Raymond-Jean Frontain and Jan Wojcik (West Lafayette, Ind.: Purdue University Press, 1980), pp. 136–53.

Ronald L. Bogue

The Twilight of Relativism: Robbe-Grillet and the Erasure of Man

The Birth of Man. Man, argues Michel Foucault in *The Order of Things*, was born at the end of the eighteenth century.[1] Not that human beings did not exist before this date, but man, as a clearly delineated object within a field of knowledge, and as the knowing subject problematically situated within discourse, has only come into being in the last two hundred years.

In what Foucault calls the Classical Age (roughly the seventeenth and eighteenth centuries), writers speak endlessly about man and human nature, but "the very concept of human nature, and the way in which it functioned," obviate "any possibility of a Classical science of man" (p. 309). The Classical age conceives of knowledge as a mathematical table of continuous and ordered entities, a space of likeness articulated into identifiable elements of even gradation and necessary relation. Nature disrupts and jumbles this tabular order through the accidents of history, but man, by representing the world to himself in transparent signs and by organizing within memory a table of these signs, untangles the confused network of nature's presentations and gives knowledge voice in discourse. Human nature can only decipher nature, however, because nature itself already forms a discourse; its "great, endless, continuous surface is printed with distinct characters, in more or less general features, in marks of identification—and, consequently, in words" (p. 310).

Man and his discourse permeate the field of knowledge, and since he is ubiquitously present in its fabric, he can not be constituted as a delimited object within it.

Man can only appear when knowledge is conceived no longer in terms of tabular order and representation, but instead in terms of what Foucault calls "the analytic of finitude." Foucault's particular task in *The Order of Things* is to uncover the epistemic foundations of the Classical sciences of natural history, the analysis of wealth and general grammar, and of their modern counterparts: biology, economics, and linguistics. These modern sciences do not rest in a single space of representation but comprise separate, self-enclosed disciplines, each organized around its own central concepts: life and organic structure (biology), labor and networks of exchange (economics), and signification and systems of signs (linguistics). Man can demarcate himself within these disciplines as a living, laboring, or speaking creature, and he can know himself as an object because each of these disciplines is constituted according to its own laws and its own principles of organization. Man confronts his own finitude in these sciences, recognizing himself as a creature whose life, labor, and speech are mere fragments of systems exterior and anterior to his particular being. Yet Foucault argues that the objects of these sciences can arise only against the background of man's own finitude: life, against the experience of one's body: labor, of one's desire; language, of one's speaking thought.

> At the foundation of all the empirical positivities, and of everything that can indicate itself as a concrete limitation of man's existence, we discover a finitude—which is in a sense the same: it is marked by the spatiality of the body, the yawning of desire, and the time of language; and yet it is radically other: in this sense, the limitation is expressed not as a determination imposed upon man from outside (because he has a nature or a history), but as a fundamental finitude

which rests on nothing but its own existence as fact, and opens
upon the positivity of all concrete limitation. (p. 315)

Foucault's basic point is perhaps most clearly indicated in *The
Birth of the Clinic*, published three years before *The Order of
Things*. It is an account of the emergence of modern clinical
medicine from 1780 to 1830—roughly contemporaneous with
the emergence of the sciences of biology, economics, and linguistics.[2] The foundation of modern medicine is to be discerned
not in man's dissipation of centuries of superstition and his ac-
cession to the clarity of empirical vision, Foucault argues, but in
a conception of death that allowed new objects of knowledge to
take form. Classificatory medicine of the Classical age conceived of death as the empty limit of life and disease, just as it
saw man's finitude as the negation of the infinite, the sign of
man's imperfection before God's perfection. In the Classical
age, disease was understood in terms of life, and life in terms of
itself. Life and disease were essences which knowledge abstracted
from the distorting accidents of the particular material body before death swallowed life and disease within its night. Modern
medicine began when death became the privileged perspective
for viewing life and disease, when man's life was defined, not in
opposition to God's being, but in relation to its own irreducible
finitude. Only when death was located at the core of life and
disease could the empirical facts of modern medicine appear.
Only when the body assumed its own particular death could it
become the space where life and disease manifested their immediate truth.

One can see, in the light of *The Order of Things*, why Foucault grants clinical medicine such importance in the formation
of the sciences of man, "an importance that is not only methodological, but ontological, in that it concerns man's being as

object of positive knowledge" (*The Birth of the Clinic*, p. 197). Here is most clearly revealed the fact that man appears as an object within knowledge only when he constitutes himself on the basis of his own finitude.

The Birth of Relativism. If by relativism we mean the belief that no absolute guarantor of truth exists, that no transcendental signified anchors discourse, that no perspective allows man to apprehend himself as an objective totality, then relativism and man came into existence at the same time. Nietzsche first announced the death of God, but it occurred before he was born, when the analytic of finitude founded man, clinical medicine, biology, economics, and linguistics. Classical knowledge was based on God. God ordered nature and inscribed in it signs of its organizational principles; God ordered man's mind and gave him a transparent discourse in which he might represent to himself the perfect superimposition of the mind's grid on the table of nature. Knowledge since the end of the eighteenth century is based on death: man's death, by which he defines his being, and God's death, implicit in man's refusal to measure his finitude against divine infinity.

Man's appearance as an entity within the field of knowledge introduces a discordant doubling of man as subject and object that raises several problems related to those of relativism. One is the problem of the *cogito* and the unconscious. Man comes to know himself through the sciences of life, labor, and language, but there he sees himself enmeshed in systems that surpass his awareness, leading him to ask: How can the *cogito* include both thought and the unthought?

How can man *be* that life whose web, pulsations, and buried energy constantly exceed the experience that he is immediately given of them? How can he *be* that labor whose laws and demands are imposed upon him like some alien system? How can he *be* the subject of a language that for thousands of years has been formed without him, a language whose organization escapes him, whose meaning sleeps an almost invincible sleep in the words he momentarily activates by means of discourse, and within which he is obliged, from the very outset, to lodge his speech and thought, as though they were doing no more than animate, for a brief period, one segment of that web of innumerable possibilities? [*The Order of Things*, p. 323]

Another is the problem of origins and history. Man seeks his origin in the archaic past of life, labor, and language, but he recognizes in each field a chronology proper to itself, and in none a chronology that is his own. Man's sense of origin is rather that of being articulated "upon the already-begun of life, labor and language . . . where man in all simplicity applies his labor to a world that has been worked for thousands of years, lives in the freshness of his unique, recent, and precarious existence a life that has its roots in the first organic formations, and composes into sentences which have never been spoken (even though generation after generation have repeated them) words that are older than all memory" (p. 330). His origin is dual, imminently present in his emergence, radically distant in the life, labor, and language that permeate him; he "is not contemporaneous with his being" (p. 335). He is dispersed across histories following their own rhythm and development, "but is himself, in his own historicity, that by means of which a history of human life, a history of economics, and a history of languages are given their form" (p. 370).

A third problem is that of the subject and discourse. Knowledge of man takes form in the sciences of life, labor, and language, but that knowledge must always be reintegrated with the subject who knows and the discourse by which he knows. The possibility of truth requires a true discourse, and "either this true discourse finds its foundation and model in the empirical truth whose genesis in nature and in history it retraces, so that one has an analysis of the positivist type (the truth of the object determines the truth of the discourse that describes its formation); or the true discourse anticipates the truth whose nature and history it defines; it sketches it out in advance and foments it from a distance, so that one has a discourse of the eschatological type (the truth of the philosophical discourse constitutes the truth in formation)" (p. 320). Yet discourse no longer possesses its Classical clarity, but exists "only in a dispersed way: for philologists, words are like so many objects formed and deposited by history; for those who wish to achieve a formalization, language must strip itself of its concrete content and leave nothing visible but those forms of discourse that are universally valid; if one's intent is to interpret, then words become a text to be broken down, so as to allow that other meaning hidden in them to emerge and become clearly visible; lastly, language may sometimes arise for its own sake in an act of writing that designates nothing other than itself" (p. 304). In language's multiplicity, in its opacity arises the possibility that discourse follows its own laws, that truth is merely its emanation.

These problems of relativism emerge with the birth of man, and they must remain problems as long as they exist in this epistemic field, for the analytic of finitude authorizes both *cogito* and unconscious, both proximate and distant origins, both language as object of knowledge and language as generator of knowledge. The dissolution of these problems lies beyond the twilight of man where one's task is "to imagine, for an instant, what the world and thought and truth might be if man did not exist" (p. 322). For literature, conceived of as language about itself, the task is to imagine language that *speaks* itself, in which man is "erased, like a face drawn in sand at the edge of the sea"

(p. 387). One writer who is attempting this task is Alain Robbe-Grillet.[3]

Men and Erasers. In Robbe-Grillet's novel *Topology of a Phantom City* (1975), the narrator, attending an opera, notices that an H has replaced the G formerly inscribed on the oriflamme of a ship onstage, and he determines to examine it further: "I grab my opera glasses in order to verify this important detail of the production (if not of the script [*du texte*]), adjust them to my orbits, and slowly turn the screw to focus the image of the inscription exactly, although this particular problem, the erasure [*gommage*] of a letter and its replacement by the one that follows it in alphabetical order, in this case effacing a G in favor of an H, was dealt with in an exhaustive fashion back in the first novel I published" (p. 98). Robbe-Grillet's first published novel, which appeared in 1953, is titled *Les Gommes (The Erasers)*, and its last words are "les hommes" (men). From G to H, from *gommes* to *hommes*: Is the relationship between men and erasers part of the problem treated so exhaustively in this novel? Or is it simply a joke: erase erasers and produce men. Perhaps a pun: the novel's protagonist is a man and "gomme" (a gumshoe, a detective); he is also a modern Oedipus (as Robbe-Grillet indicates explicitly throughout the novel), modeled after Western literature's original detective who solved the riddle of man but did not know himself.[4] The novel's protagonist, named Wallas, seeks in several stationery stores an eraser like one he had seen before, but whose brand name he could not decipher since only the central two letters of the manufacturer's name, "di," remained uneffaced on the eraser's surface. Though he does not know it, the eraser bears the trace of his mythic identity: Oedipe. A sign of Wallas's self-ignorance, the eraser he seeks is also a sign of himself: something "soft, light, friable, which pressure does not deform but reduces to dust" (*The Erasers*, p. 132), an instrument of negation in the process of regular self-disintegration. Man as eraser: an emptiness with shape that resolves itself into dust.

Men and erasers are also linked by desire. Whenever Wallas asks a salesgirl for an eraser, an incipient eroticism pervades the scene.[5] The eraser is an intermediary of desire, but perhaps also itself an object of desire, not simply for Wallas, but for all men. Men love erasers because they remove mistakes, blemishes and failures, they correct texts, they expunge the undesirable. The narrator of Robbe-Grillet's third novel, *Jealousy* (1957), fears that his wife is unfaithful and symbolically projects his anxieties onto a spot on the wall in his home left by a centipede which his wife's lover had squashed. Midway through the novel, the narrator finds an eraser and tries to remove from the wall "the suspect trace" of the centipede so that, at most, it will "pass for an insignificant defect of the surface" (p. 131). In trying to efface this sign of the unknown, the question-mark-shaped stain of the centipede, in trying to exorcise the wife and passion that exceed his grasp, the narrator is merely doing what he does when he obsessively enumerates and measures the elements of his domain: attempting to impose a form on his world, to gain control, to write his master text.

Thus erasure is a form of writing[6]—or perhaps the truth of writing, in that most writing is an erasure of awareness of the unwritten. This truth eludes most seekers of truth, for they are possessed by the will to truth, which is the companion of the will to power. The will to power shapes a text that passes for truth; the will to truth then seeks to confirm the text and to enforce the text's power. Oedipus, like most detectives, devotes himself to the will to truth—indeed, he sacrifices himself to it. So does Wallas, but his fate unmasks the will to truth. Wallas seeks the murderer of a man named Dupont, but Dupont has actually only been wounded by the assassin's bullet and has decided to fake his own death. Wallas, suspecting that the killer

will return to Dupont's house, waits there in ambush for him—
but Dupont returns instead, and Wallas unwittingly kills him.
Like Oedipus, Wallas is both murderer and detective, but while
Oedipus uncovers a pre-existent truth, Wallas creates truth.
Truth is made, not found—to which truth the will to truth is
constitutionally blind.

Man is an ignorant detective seeking an external truth which
he forms in his texts, which, at their origin, and with no antecedents, are emendations, omissions, and corrections. Man is unable to recognize himself in these texts, perhaps because he fears
he will discover himself to be a creature defined by his annihila-
tion, an object of knowledge in the process of self-disintegration.

Man is an eraser.

Beyond Humanism: The Erasure of Man, Time, and Space.
In *For a New Novel*, a collection of essays written between 1955
and 1963, Robbe-Grillet fights the imposition on fiction of a
particular conception of man that one may label "humanist"
(following his terminology in the essay "Nature, Humanism,
Tragedy"). The humanist view of man was expressed by realistic
novelists of the nineteenth century, who characterized him as a
coherent and knowable creature inhabiting a world permeated
with human significance and living within a time that is uniform, linear, and shaped by an inherent teleology. Traditional
fiction demands that man have a name, family, heredity, profes-
sion, possessions and "a 'character,' a face that reflects it, a past
which has shaped that face and that character" (p. 27)—in short,
a human nature. The narration of his life "must flow without
jolts, as if by itself, with that irrepressible *élan* that secures our
adherence at once" (p. 30). His world must reflect his emotions, afford him unity with nature, and give him "a certain
predestination" (p. 51) by providing landscapes with qualities
that anticipate the individual and his feelings. Robbe-Grillet
wants instead to separate man and nature, "to affirm that there

exists something, in the world, which is not man, which addresses no sign to him, which has nothing in common with him" (p. 47). He wants to deprive time of "its character of certitude, its tranquility, its innocence" (p. 32). And he wants to imagine characters who are not constantly explained, but who exist only with an impenetrable *Dasein*: "Whereas the traditional hero is constantly solicited, absorbed, destroyed by these interpretations which the author offers, projected ceaselessly into an immaterial and unstable *elsewhere*, always more distant, always more blurred, the future hero, on the contrary, will remain *there*" (p. 21).

Clearly, Robbe-Grillet's is a limited attack on man in *For a New Novel*, and in his novels of the 1950s his major characters maintain a certain minimal coherence. In *The Voyeur* and *Jealousy* Robbe-Grillet plays with readers' desires for authorial analysis of characters by presenting abnormal protagonists (a psychopathic killer and an obsessively jealous husband) without hinting at the causes of their peculiarities. Yet by using a limited third-person point of view (in *The Voyeur*) and an "absent-I" point of view (in *Jealousy*), he creates the impression that the consciousness of a single subject with a possible extratextual existence is being represented through language.[7]

Any residue of a natural, transtextual character is absent, however, in *La Maison de rendez-vous* (1965) and the novels written thereafter. One can never be sure in *La Maison de rendez-vous* whether the slight changes in the spelling of characters' names indicate the presence of different characters: Is the same person designated by Lady Ava, Eva, Eve, Eva Bergmann? Or by Lauren, Laureen, Loraine B.? Or Johnson, Ralph Johnson, Sir Ralph (known as "the American")? Is Sir Ralph related to the nineteenth-century sculptor Johnson, Jonstone, or R. Jonestone, or the playwright Jonestone who wrote *The Murder of Edouard Manneret*? And if the name remains the same, as in the case of Edouard Manneret, is the same person being referred to? Is Edouard Manneret a writer, the painter of the famous *Maya*, a drug dealer, a senile drug addict, a loan shark, a sexual maniac who conducts nefarious experiments on drugged girls, a "doctor, chemist and something of a fetishist" addicted to "vampirism and necrophilia" (p. 167), or a double agent for the Formosa government?

The characters of *La Maison de rendez-vous* seem mere shifting façades, players disguised beneath changing masks; in *Project for a Revolution in New York* (1970) Robbe-Grillet makes explicit the relationship of characters to masks. Early in the novel the narrator describes a wig and mask shop specializing in masks so realistic that their artificial nature cannot be detected; after that, the reader is forced to suspect that all characters are wearing masks. (Indeed, masks are so much a part of the characters that one man, in removing his mask, tears away large pieces of his flesh [p. 61].) Ben-Saïd, for instance, is identified as one of the masked figures loading marijuana cigarettes into a Buick (p. 72), but he is also supposed to be the mysterious figure, poorly disguised as a stereotypical detective, staking out the narrator's house (p. 104). Later this detective is designated as "the fake Ben-Saïd" (p. 114), while "the true Ben-Saïd" (p. 125) is located on a subway car (although twenty-two pages later this subway rider is called "the false Ben-Saïd"). Finally, a bald "locksmith voyeur" (p. 195), summoned to the narrator's house by the stake-out detective Ben-Saïd, enters the house, copulates with a dead girl in the library, and then "removes the mask of the bald locksmith which covered his head and face, gradually unsticking the layer of plastic material and revealing, little by little, in its place the features of the true Ben-Saïd" (p. 198). And if "the true Ben-Saïd" is a mask?

A collection of masks, a bundle of clichés and stereotypes: this is man in the later novels of Robbe-Grillet—unbelievable and preposterous. (Can anyone take seriously Lady G. in *Memories of the Golden Triangle* [1978] who says "On my identity card, my maiden name is Caroline de Saxe, but my true name is Belzebeth, princess of the blood, more often named the bloody princess" [p. 154]?) The characters in these novels are mere scraps of text that emerge from and dissolve into the narrative without even a fixed relation to the narrative itself. The narrator's position is occupied by various characters who refer to the text from an authorial perspective, while "the narrator" serves merely as the designation of another character in the narrative. (One narrator in *Topology of a Phantom City* breaks off a description of a scene because his view is blocked by "the head of the narrator" [p. 36].) The narrator's "I" indicates no individual identity, simply the activation of a roving shifter that constitutes a temporary subject. The characters have no stable relation to the narrative because they are mere projections of language, their identities constructed from texts—a fact made explicit in *Memories of the Golden Triangle* when, in the midst of a third-person narrative, a subject emerges from the text as if in linguistic autogenesis: "The man is alone, in the silence, in the middle of the cell. And little by little, as if with prudence, I observe that it is I, probably" (p. 41). In Robbe-Grillet's later fiction, man has no substance, no presence, no autonomy. He is merely a text-effect.

The humanist time of nineteenth-century realism, the time of regular chronological progression, of a recuperable past and a partially predictable future, is undermined by Robbe-Grillet in his first three published novels by his explorations of subjective, psychological time, with its hesitations, repetitions, projections, fantasies, and fixations. But already in *The Erasers* one can discern the possibility of other forms of time, neither objective nor subjective, the property of neither the collectivity nor the individual. Time is suspended in *The Erasers* (Wallas's watch stops

for twenty-four hours and starts again when he kills Dupont);
time repeats itself (Wallas's actions precisely double many of
those of the unsuccessful assassin who precedes him); yet this
repetition creates new events of unexpected displacements (there
are, says Robbe-Grillet in his résumé of the novel on the back
cover, "twenty-four hours in excess"). This is the time of dislo-
cated repetition, of the return of the *Unheimliche*, the same that
is other.

Robbe-Grillet supplies a fit image of this time in "Le chemin
du retour" (The Way Back; more literally, The Path of Return),
a short text written in 1954 and published in *Snapshots*. Three
men cross a jetty from the mainland to an island and try to circle
the island before the tide rises and covers the jetty. The story
opens in the past tense, with the men sighting a mainland marker
that indicates that they have completed the island circuit; then it
shifts to the present tense to relate their journey around the island. When they again reach the mainland marker, the past
tense is resumed—yet any certainty of return, promised at the
story's inception, disappears as the men observe unexpected and
unsettling alterations in the landscape. The jetty (the same jetty?
another one?) is covered with water, and a hitherto unnoticed
old man offers them a ride in a rowboat. At the story's conclusion the three men sit helplessly in the boat as the deaf old man
rows obliquely toward some unknown destination. The path of
return exceeds the mark; the present does not match up with the
past. The time of return is a loss of origin, a cycle that spins out
of control.

Discordant repetition plays a major role in Robbe-Grillet's
fourth novel, *In the Labyrinth* (1959), which recounts the wan-
derings of a soldier through a ghostly city in search of someone
to whom he is supposed to give a package. He meets a child, he
follows the child, he is followed by the child, he meets the child
(again?), he is led by the child to a dark hallway, or a family's

apartment, or a café, or a military hospital, he does not follow the child, etc.—and with no explanation of the temporal relations of these events or of their incongruities and contradictions. The soldier inhabits a labyrinth of forking paths, choosing no single course of action but following several possible destinies, the time of each destiny coexisting with the others. Robbe-Grillet allows the recuperation of this splintered time within a conventional time by suggesting that the novel's confusing events represent the thoughts of an author in the process of inventing a novel—trying out various plot possibilities, rejecting some, pursuing others, until a coherent story is fashioned and the labyrinth is solved. In *La Maison de rendez-vous*, however, he offers no solution to the plot's labyrinth of disjunctions and recurrences, but presents an unmediated serial time of slightly differing repetitions, of discrepant returns and reticulating dispersions. Rather than growing more coherent, events become more convoluted and improbable. The novel closes with the network of temporal inferences tangled and knotted.

Serial time predominates in the novels written after *La Maison de rendez-vous*, but in increasingly complicated and problematic ways. In *La Maison de rendez-vous* temporal incongruities exist between various scenes, but within the individual scenes time remains relatively coherent. The temporal span within which the scenes occur is also fairly limited, suggesting that the time of the narrative as a whole can be subsumed within rational time. But in *Topology of a Phantom City*, for example, the units of temporal coherence are greatly diminished, perhaps reaching their nadir during the section entitled "Ritual Ceremony," when a young girl awaits her murderer who is climbing the stairs to her room: "He readjusts, on the belt of his uniform jacket, the knife with the broad blade which lies at present on the black and white marble floor, at the foot of the divan, near the red stain whose area is enlarging, in the naked room where already the day is sinking, where the corners darken, where the attentive girl continues to brush with care her long golden hair, her sense on the alert, her mind elsewhere" (p. 161). The temporal dislocations of *Topology* extend without limit, for the action stretches over centuries, from a mythic past to an indefinite present. The phantom city is an archeological site in which the ruins of various eras are preserved in jumbled and unpredictable juxtaposition, but in which any level can come to life as narratives from various temporal strata intersect, combine, and fuse with one another. Time is as topologically enigmatic as space in the novel, its most appropriate single image being the temple inscription which records the destruction of the city following a volcanic eruption, written in cuneiform characters which historians have determined disappeared three centuries before the disaster occurred—a "chronological contradiction" which "no one has yet resolved" (p. 42).

The temporal disjunctions of repetition find their simplest expression in "Le chemin du retour," and in "Retour raturé" (Return Erased), a section of *Topology* (pp. 149–56), perhaps their most complex. In "Retour raturé" a return also runs out of control, tangentially askew, but only after the narrator has stated four times (in the *passé composé*) that he has returned home "as always" ("comme chaque fois"). The final time he describes his return he passes through a ruined city, when before him appear (where?) alternating images of three eggs and four or five fighting men, until at the close of the text the eggs explode and the previous returns are erased. Interspersed between the four statements of the narrator's return are three scenes that form a serial sequence (one in the present tense, two in the imperfect). (1) The narrator sees in the water of a quay several pieces of paper amid other garbage, and then he returns home. (2) The narrator gathers some of the sheets of paper, tries unsuccessfully to read them in the dim light, rolls the pages into a ball, throws them in the quay, and returns home. (3) The narrator reads the pages, rolls them into a ball, throws them in the quay, and returns home. Each of these contradictory returns erases the others; each one concludes with a marker of indefinite repetition: "comme chaque fois." The return takes place at night, but the time of narration is made uncertain in the opening lines: "It is morning. It is evening. I remember" (p. 149). Is it the morning after return, or the evening before? Or both at once? Later, all hope of resolving the question disappears when the narrator states, "It is morning, it is evening, I no longer know, and the uncertain light outside furnishes no clarification on this point" (p. 153). Even the cycle of night and day, sleeping and awaking is rendered problematic, for the narrator's sleep represents a temporal gap of unknowable dimensions: "I must have slept a long time, doubtlessly a very long time, an indeterminable time, a blank time [*un temps mort*]. I remember nothing, as usual" (p. 153). Contradictory sequences, ceaseless repetition, indistinct cycles, limitless gaps—all form the fabric of an inhuman time, a purely textual time.

Deformations of space are as thorough as those of time in Robbe-Grillet's later fiction—and they are perhaps more striking, since Robbe-Grillet was best known early in his career for his passionless, mathematical descriptions of objects which, although they lacked depth and resonance with human sensibilities, nevertheless existed within a coherent space. Minute descriptions of physical space persist in the novels after *In the Labyrinth*, but the relation between the spaces described becomes enigmatic, shifting, and contradictory. Rooms communicate with one another in impossible configurations; stairways have more flights descending than ascending; buildings possess problematic dimensions, with more stories, hallways, and rooms than their external appearances would allow; neighborhoods disappear and reappear somewhere else; landmarks are sited in more than one location. Robbe-Grillet further undermines spatial stability by melding the worlds of reality, dream, and art. In *Topology*, for instance, a woman dreams of ancient inscriptions that instigate a narrative (first introduced as a scene on a Tarot card) that proves to be an opera, a tableau which the narrator details until his description of a Tarot card in the hand of one of the actresses turns into a narrative of a woman and two children who are viewing the opera theater from a distant tower, and who subsequently descend a stairway inside the tower, stop midway in their descent to look out through a window on the opera audience, and emerge finally on the empty stage of the vacant theater. The trajectory of such texts, through shifting topographies and conflicting planes of reality, delineates a space that is purely its own, subsumable within no human perspective whether objective, subjective, or oneiric.

Man's world is in gradual disintegration in Robbe-Grillet's fiction, and the course of its dissolution can be traced in the images of the city in his works. The city of *The Erasers* is a grim Flemish town of dutiful workers, unremarkable public edifices, and identical office buildings resembling adding machines and stacks of ledgers. *In the Labyrinth* takes place in an eerie city of endlessly duplicated façades, depopulated before its imminent occupation by enemy soldiers. The Hong Kong of *La Maison de rendez-vous* offers an urban landscape more colorful and busy than those of the earlier novels, but it is clearly a collage of stereotypes from thriller novels and travel posters, whose origins are betrayed by the inordinate piles of trash that litter its streets. Robbe-Grillet's New York in *Project for a Revolution in New York* is also a composite of popular myths, but myths of a city fast approaching total destruction. Late in the novel the narrator asks, "Have I already indicated that, even before the revolution, the entire city of New York, in particular the island of Manhattan, had been in ruins for a long time?" (p. 207). The city's destruction is virtually complete in *Topology of a Phantom City*, its streets populated solely with spectres and apparitions. Equally phantom are the inhabitants of the city of *Memories of the Golden Triangle*, equally unreal and unworldly its juxtaposition of cultures, histories, and geographical features. The city is covered with "vast zones in demolition" (p. 32), and its perimeter is "tacitly abandoned to marginal types, drug addicts and perverts, rebels who oppose all control, as well as promoters of future constructions" (p. 31). The cities of Robbe-Grillet's last two novels, these constructions in ruins, are metaphors of the text itself, but also signs of man's demise. In these novels one senses an author alone, at play with phantoms who prowl the jumbled fragments of a time and space long since abandoned by men.

Still one must ask: Isn't the author a man? Mustn't he be erased?

The Death of the Sovereign. In *The Order of Things*, Foucault uses Velázquez's *Las Meninas* to illustrate man's relation to knowledge in the Classical age. The painting depicts Velázquez at work before a canvas, and beside him the Infanta Margarita and her entourage of courtiers and dwarfs. Velázquez looks out of the painting towards what must be the subject of the painting within the painting: King Philip IV and his wife, whose presence is indicated only by a reflection in a mirror on the wall behind Velázquez. The painting represents representation, and the focus of all elements in the painting is the position in front of the canvas occupied by the King—and by the viewer of *Las Meninas*. In Classical, representational knowledge, man is the sovereign who structures the portrait of order but never appears in the painting.

When man enters the picture, the king becomes threatened. Man is doubled, and the monarch who surveys grows confused with the subject who obeys. The novelist's temptation is to make this newly created man the object of an exhaustive portrait and to assume himself the position of the sovereign—certainly the divine posture Balzac affects in writing the *Comédie humaine*. This is a double temptation: to ignore the contradictions inherent in man's constitution by portraying him as complete and coherent, and to deny that one is a man. But can one be both a man and an author? Can one commit regicide and not commit suicide?

In Robbe-Grillet's first novel, *A Regicide*, written in 1949 but not published until 1978, an unstable factory statistician named Boris (after Moussorgsky's mad king and regicide, Boris Godunov[8]) attempts to kill his King. The King is a genial government figurehead whose assassination would change nothing, but Boris becomes increasingly elated as he plans the King's murder and senses a new purpose to his life. He starts to feel a hidden bond with the King, and when he imagines the scene of the regicide, the King looks at Boris with the knowing complicity of one who welcomes his death, greeting him as if the two shared a secret kinship. The interpenetration of dream and reality in the story makes it difficult to tell whether Boris actually kills the King, but by the end of the novel Boris's elation has disappeared as he senses that his mission has failed.

Parallel to the third-person narrative of Boris is a first-person narrative, which alternates with the Boris narrative and occasionally merges with it, of a man on an otherworldly island covered with a perpetual fog. As Boris plans the regicide, the man on the island begins to encounter a magician named Malus, reputed to exist only in legend. The man follows Malus, and gradually Malus transforms the island into a spring garden. The beautiful sirens swim ashore, and the man makes love with one of them. Yet Malus warns him not to stay with the sirens, and when they begin to swim away from the island it becomes clear that his siren lover is beckoning him to his death, for he cannot breathe underwater as she can. The narrator stays behind when the sirens depart, and by the novel's end his island is again shrouded in fog.

The sovereign author in the modern world is a weak, pathetic figure who deserves, and calls for, his own destruction. The writer's battle with this figure may seem useless and mad, but it is crucial for his existence, even though it is unsettling and threatening, since he recognizes himself in the King. The author in the age of myth and belief created as a god, transforming the world, as does Malus. But his name now means "evil one": the omnipotent author can now summon only destructive sirens. The once powerful and now decrepit sovereign must be killed. Yet by the end of A *Regicide* Boris has failed, and the island narrator is sunk in his solitary fog.

Boris reappears in *La Maison de rendez-vous* as the name of a mad king who is never seen but only heard, banging his cane on the floor of the apartment above the narrator (or, more correctly, narrators). The central event of the novel is the death of Edouard Manneret, who is first introduced as a writer and who is later connected with Boris. When Ralph Johnson goes to Manneret to ask for a loan, he finds "the Old Man," as he is often called, in a rocking chair (elsewhere in the text associated with Boris [pp. 161, 209]) with a look on his face of "a child or a madman" (p. 114). Manneret mistakes Johnson for his son, and when Johnson gives his name, Manneret mocks him by saying, "'And I'm king Boris'" (p. 114). Several versions of Manneret's death are reported, but his murder is only directly described once, at the end of the novel, when Ralph Johnson shoots Manneret as he rocks in his chair.

The creator of *La Maison de rendez-vous* is doubled in the novel: the writer Manneret, whose death produces the text, and the sovereign author Boris, an annoying old madman who demands recognition, pounding like the superego on the ceiling of the narrator's skull. When Johnson shoots his "father" (the writer, the author of his being), we must conclude that he kills both Manneret and Boris.

Yet someone keeps tapping on the ceiling in *Project for a Revolution in New York*, trying to send messages to other inhabitants of the house: "Who is tapping, with little light, sharp blows, in the blind room of the last story, at the top of the big house? You're not going to claim that it is old king Boris?" (p. 209). Apparently the old fool is hard to kill, and perhaps for this reason he is given his own proper death in *Memories of the Golden Triangle*. At an opera the narrator meets Vanessa, who tells the story of "the death of the king Charles-Boris, called Boris of the blue beard." (Three pages later her narrative is identified as the last act of an opera subtitled "A Regicide" [p. 95].) He is "the last king" (p. 93), awaiting the arrival of revolutionaries in his palace. He sits at his desk with its "many erasers, pencils and pen-holders of all sorts, mostly useless," trying to repair a chip in the desk's veneer. When the revolutionaries enter the palace, he greets them "as would a father on the arrival of his children" (p. 94) and assumes an official pose to make it easier for the revolutionaries to kill him. They fire, and "the old sovereign falls riddled with bullets" (p. 95).

The promise of A *Regicide* is fulfilled: the king is dead. The sovereign author will no longer try to repair his useless craft; instead, he will aid his children in their textual revolution. The question now is, How does one kill an author?

Visible Erasure. One of Edouard Manneret's manuscript pages, "three-quarters covered with a very small writing, regular and close, without erasure" (p. 71), ends with the unfinished sentence "'would relate [*raconterait*], on his return from a trip [*voyage*]'" (p. 72). A servant girl's hand, resting on the manuscript, points at the word "represents." Somewhat later Manneret resumes his work: "after the word 'trip,' he writes the adjective

'secret' and stops again" (p. 76). This is an oblique characteriza-
tion of traditional, representational literature: the author em-
barks on the secret journey of the process of artistic creation,
and on his return he recounts stories without erasure, bearing
no trace of the process of their formation. But Manneret alters
his text: "Edouard Manneret, at his work table, erases [*gomme*]
with care the word 'secret,' so that no trace of it remains on the
sheet of paper, then he writes in its place the words 'to distant
places' [*lointain*]" (p. 83). This is the change Robbe-Grillet proposes: to abandon the kind of writing that treats the writer's creative labor as a means to an end, and to make his *voyage lointain* toward a text the subject of the text itself. No trace of Manneret's erasure remains on the page, because the concepts of
correction and mistake no longer exist. (After all, isn't Manneret's erasure of "secret" *in* the text?) Every page is without
erasure, not because the text has been corrected and rewritten,
but because all the writer's false starts, hesitations, contradictions, and dead ends *comprise* the text.

To what *voyage lointain* in particular does Manneret's text refer? To *La Maison de rendez-vous*, with its "improbable stories
of Oriental journeys [*voyages en Orient*—a salute to Nerval], with
pimp antique dealers, white-slave trade, too skillful dogs, broth-
els for perverts, drug traffic and mysterious murders" (p. 106).
As Lady Eva says, all these tales of the Blue Villa, Lauren, Johnson, and Manneret "are stories invented by *voyageurs*" (p. 187).
(Robbe-Grillet also alludes here to *The Voyeur*, whose protagonist is often referred to as a salesman, *un voyageur*.) Yet these
stories are not frivolous or haphazard. The final version of Manneret's page reads "'trip to distant places, and not gratuitous, but
necessary'" (p. 176). The writer's *voyage lointain* is necessary
because it follows an internal logic, but also because it is the
writer's only option once he has decided to kill the author—an

act which is, as the police lieutenant says of the murder of Manneret, a "'necesary crime and not gratuitous'" (p. 68).

One kills the author by making him not invisible, but more
visible. *In the Labyrinth* is Robbe-Grillet's first novel which in-
corporates the writer's process of shaping a text in the text itself.
The writer's deliberations about the sequence of plot events, the
verisimilitude of the actions, or the relationships of the characters to one another merge with the narrative of the soldier wan-
dering the city streets. If a series of events leads to an impasse,
an abrupt "No" brings the series to a halt and inaugurates a new
one. The source of the writer's invention is also described in the
text: an engraving titled "The Defeat of Reichenfels," to which
the writer periodically returns for new plot ideas. Hence one
can follow in the novel the development of the writer's plot from
its inception to its completed résumé in the closing pages of the
book.

In novels after *In the Labyrinth* Robbe-Grillet abandons this
kind of writer within the text; along with it he abandons the
illusion that the text *represents* his consciousness. (Of course,
writers appear quite often in the later novels, but never as the
controlling mind that shapes the entire text.) The drive toward a
coherent solution of plot difficulties also disappears, and emphasis falls on devices like the engraving of "The Defeat of Reichenfels," which Robbe-Grillet labels "generators": images, objects,
concepts or words that instigate textual production and that the
text itself refers to.[9] The color red, for instance, is a central generator in *Project for a Revolution in New York*,[10] and the major
themes generated from it are stated in the text when the narrator
attends a revolutionary meeting during which three actors take
turns delivering speeches: "The theme of the day's lecture seems
to be 'the color red,' envisioned as a radical solution to the irreducible antagonism between black and white. Each of the three

voices is devoted, at present, to one of the major liberating actions related to red: rape, arson, murder" (p. 38). Black, white, rape, arson, murder, and revolution subsequently become subjects of the narrative and serve in turn as generators of other themes. Robbe-Grillet presents the generators of *Topology of a Phantom City* in an even more direct manner, titling the opening chapter of the first part "In the Generative Cell," the cell itself being a prison cell in which young women engage in various symbolic activities, and the procreative cell from which the organism of the text springs. Later in the novel the narrator interrupts a description of the oriflamme of a ship to state that the letter G on the oriflamme (in combination with elements generated earlier in the text) "gives the following series": "vanadé-vigie-navire/danger-rivage-devin/nager-en vain-carnage/divan-vierge-vagin/gravide-engendra-david" (Vanadé-look-out-ship/danger-shore-soothsayer/swim-in vain-carnage/divan-virgin-vagina/pregnant-engendered-david [p. 49]). This phonologically generated series is then followed by a narrative based on the series.

In his essay "On the Choice of Generators," Robbe-Grillet states that he looks on the generators themselves not as creations of an autonomous imagination, but as materials supplied by the social world for his fashioning.[11] No innocent utilization of language is possible, he believes, since all the customs, practices, power relations, and modes of knowledge of a particular society permeate a language. He cannot create generators that escape cultural determination, so he deliberately chooses popular myths, clichés, stereotypes, and previously formed texts as generators: "If you wish, to take up again the celebrated opposition of Saussure, I do not work on the *langue* (this French of the twentieth century which I utilize as I have received it) but on the *parole* of a society (this discourse which is addressed to me by the world

in which I live)" (p. 160). He seems to have reached an understanding of language similar to Barthes' understanding of the
text in "The Death of the Author": "We know now that a text is
not a line of words releasing a single 'theological' meaning (the
'message' of the Author-God) but a multi-dimensional space in
which a variety of writings, none of them original, blend and
clash. The text is a tissue of quotations drawn from the innumerable centers of culture." [12] Robbe-Grillet's strategy is to accept
the social texts which surround him, break them into pieces,
and then reassemble them in a different pattern.

In *La Maison de rendez-vous* Robbe-Grillet works with the
Hong Kong of the popular imagination, in *Project* with modern
fantasies and phobias about New York, and in *Topology of a Phantom City* and *Memories of the Golden Triangle* with Western
culture's obsession with the figure of the raped virgin. [13] But in
Topology and *Golden Triangle* he further emphasizes the intertextual nature of his enterprise by using as generators works by
other artists: photographs by David Hamilton and Irina Ionesco,
etchings by Paul Delvaux and Robert Rauschenberg, paintings
by René Magritte, paintings, prints, and sculptures by Jasper
Johns. In fact, most of *Topology* and much of *Golden Triangle*
appeared first in separate publications, each accompanied by il-
lustrations of the artworks that generated the particular text. [14]
Thus these novels, besides alluding generally to cultural myths,
point directly to their genesis in sources outside the text.

In developing texts from these generators, he never uses the
generators as Rorschach blots, but explores only those networks
of association established in and by cultural codes. Robbe-Grillet's
generative practices have aptly been likened to those of Freudian
dream-work, [15] but one must remember that the metaphoric
condensations and metonymic displacements of the text are not
unconscious and private, but conscious and public. Indeed,

only because the generative process is public can one follow its unfolding in the text, identify its sources, and recover its rules of formation.

What, then, is left of the author? He gathers pre-existent myths, texts and image clusters, fragments them, and sets them in motion. He activates language, letting it speak itself, trace the path of its speaking, and speak about its own speaking. Yet this speech, because fragmented, assumes an unusual opacity, an alien cadence and tone which forces man to face the otherness inherent in the texts that constitute him.

The author does build texts, but he mocks the rage for order that impels him to create. Robbe-Grillet makes constructions in ruins—constructions composed of cultural shards, constructions in the process of self-annihilation and dissolution. The narrator of *Memories of the Golden Triangle* is shown objects which he must incorporate into narratives, given items which he must arrange in an organizational scheme, and brought before tableaux with unvoiced problems which he must solve. He succeeds, but in ludicrous ways, forming increasingly improbable narratives, placing objects in brilliantly ingenious but gratuitous patterns, and finding solutions that lead only to new problems. The narrator serves the text, his solutions answering one problem alone— that of keeping the text going. At the end of *Memories of the Golden Triangle* the narrator can only ask, "What have I said? What have I done?" (p. 237). Hidden interrogators try to force the narrator to be coherent by questioning his inconsistencies and interrupting his digressions ("'Textual error! Punishment'" [p. 155] shouts a voice at one point), but to no avail. When they demand a synopsis of the narrative at the end of the novel, the narrator complies by providing a regular and precise timetable of events. His reprise of themes and actions from the novel, however, only introduces more complications and new material.

In Robbe-Grillet's fiction only one inquisitor gets what he

wants: the police interrogator in *Project for a Revolution in New York*, whose motto is "Truth, my one passion" (p. 101) and whose method is to torture those whom he interrogates until they give all possible answers (both true and false) to his questions. This truth Robbe-Grillet's narratives offer: a meaningless truth indistinguishable from the indifferent expanse of discursive possibilities.

Lecture/Rature. Robbe-Grillet claims a political dimension to his generative fiction, arguing that his choice of popular myths as generators betrays "no submission to the codes of established society—no more to a code of values than to a narrative code—but instead a labor of deconstruction on elements cut out from the code, designated as mythological, dated, situated, non-natural, brought into broad daylight instead of bathing imperceptibly in their original plasma" ("On the Choice of Generators," p. 161). He seeks to undo ideology (which he generally equates with myth) by exposing it and breaking it into pieces, for "in order to function correctly in society, ideology needs to be masked to hide its artificiality, and needs as well to be continuous, since ideology can only function as a totality."[16] Robbe-Grillet believes that he can offer his readers a certain freedom through the text, an awareness of the arbitrary and constructed nature of social reality. He does not practice a "pure" textualism, deforming codes simply to emphasize the artificial nature of his works, creating abstract, self-referential linguistic forms which exist in a realm protected from base reality.[17] His activation of language, deconstruction of myth, and dissolution of man, time, and space represent more than assertions that his novels are mere words; for the language that he brings to speech is the reader's language, the myths that he dismembers saturate the reader's world, and the images of man, time, and space that he fractures are images the reader lives.

Robbe-Grillet also offers more strictly literary lessons by setting traps in his novels for naïve readers. He sees in his later novels "a certain bipolarity between novelistic elements and a form of writing which combat[s] them."[18] The naïve reader who anticipates representational fiction, a progressive unity and order in the text, stable characters, temporal continuity, spatial coherence, and clear authorial control finds his expectations partially fulfilled but then frustrated as the traditional novelistic elements disintegrate. Yet the text offers the reader a new role in place of the old: that of reconstructing the course of the text's generation. Thus Robbe-Grillet's novels process their own readers, erasing traditional readers and replacing them with generative readers.

In "The Death of the Author" Barthes argues that the author's demise marks the birth of the reader, a reader "without history, biography, psychology; he is simply that *someone* who holds together in a single field all the traces by which the text is constituted" (p. 148). Robbe-Grillet's novels anticipate such a reader and try to create him; but such a reader is not a man, and his birth can occur only in the wake of man's disappearance. Is Robbe-Grillet forming new readers or simply destroying the old ones? It is no more possible to know this than to know whether his erasure of man belongs at the end of one era or the beginning of another. Perhaps he writes under erasure, to use Heidegger's phrase, inscribing the words of a moribund culture, crossing them out and letting stand both the words and their negation. But perhaps at an end is the twilight of man and of the problems of relativism, and in the erasure of man speaks some new, unnameable being.

Notes

1. *The Order of Things*, trans. Alan Sheridan (New York: Vintage, 1970).

2. *The Birth of the Clinic*, trans. A. M. Sheridan Smith (New York: Vintage, 1973).

3. Robbe-Grillet has written nine novels, one group of short texts, and one collection of essays; he has also written the script of one film, written and directed six others, and published *ciné-romans* of three of his films. I am restricting my attention to his novels, short texts, and essays:

    Les Gommes [*The Erasers*] (1953; rpt. Paris: Éditions de Minuit, 1963)

    Le Voyeur [*The Voyeur*] (Paris: Éditions de Minuit, 1955)

    La Jalousie [*Jealousy*] (Paris: Éditions de Minuit, 1957)

    Dans le labyrinthe [*In the Labyrinth*] (Paris: Éditions de Minuit, 1959)

    Instantanés [*Snapshots*; short texts written between 1953 and 1962] (Paris: Éditions de Minuit, 1962)

    Pour un nouveau roman [*For a New Novel*; essays written between 1955 and 1963] (Paris: Éditions de Minuit, 1963)

    La Maison de rendez-vous (Paris: Éditions de Minuit, 1965)

    Projet pour une révolution à New York [*Project for a Revolution in New York*] (Paris: Éditions de Minuit, 1970)

    Topologie d'une cité fantôme [*Topology of a Phantom City*] (Paris: Éditions de Minuit, 1975)

    Souvenirs du triangle d'or [*Memories of the Golden Triangle*] (Paris: Éditions de Minuit, 1978)

    Un Régicide [*A Regicide*; written in 1949, first published in 1978] (Paris: Éditions de Minuit, 1978)

    All page references are to these editions and are included in the text. All translations are my own.

4. On the Oedipus theme in *Les Gommes*, see Bruce Morrissette, *The Novels of Robbe-Grillet*, rev. and aug. ed. (Ithaca: Cornell University Press, 1975), pp. 38–74; Olga Bernal, *Alain Robbe-Grillet: le roman de l'absence* (Paris: Gallimard, 1964); and Jean Alter, *La Vision du monde d'Alain Robbe-Grillet* (Genève: Droz, 1966).

5. See Morrissette, *Novels of Robbe-Grillet*, pp. 63–66.

6. One might make the same point, on a different level, in speaking of Robbe-Grillet's second novel, *The Voyeur* (1955). A watch

salesman tortures and murders a young girl and then tries to remove all signs of his crime. The crime, however, is never narrated; it is a blank in the text. The reader comes to know of it only
through the killer's efforts to obliterate its traces. He is, one might
say, a writing eraser.

7. On point of view in *Le Voyeur* and *La Jalousie*, see Morrissette,
Novels of Robbe-Grillet, pp. 75–152.

8. Robbe-Grillet makes this identification himself: "The word Boris
has appeared with a certain frequency in my texts, and it seems
that, on several occasions, extremely precise allusions have been
made, if not to the drama of Pushkin, at least to the opera of
Moussorgsky." *Robbe-Grillet: Analyse, Théorie*, Colloque de Cerisy
(Paris: Éditions 10/18, 1976), 2: 47.

9. Robbe-Grillet has objected to the use of phonemes as generators
in "Sur le choix des générateurs," *Nouveau roman: hier, au-
jourd'hui*, Colloque de Cerisy, ed. Jean Ricardou and Françoise
Rossum-Guyon (Paris: Éditions 10/18, 1972), 2: 160. Since that
statement, however, Robbe-Grillet has clearly made use of pho-
nemic generators, as Thomas O'Donnell notes in "Robbe-Grillet's
'Metaphoricité Fantôme,'" *Studies in Twentieth-Century Literature* 2 (1977): 55–68.

10. On generators in *Project for a Revolution in New York*, see Jean
Ricardou, "La Fiction flamboyante," in *Pour une théorie du Nou-
veau Roman* (Paris: Éditions du Seuil, 1971), pp. 211–33, and
Thomas O'Donnell, "Thematic Generation in Robbe-Grillet's
Projet pour une révolution à New York," in *Twentieth-Century
French Fiction: Essays Presented to Germaine Brée*, ed. George
Stambolian (New Brunswick, N.J.: Rutgers University Press,
1975), pp. 184–97.

11. Robbe-Grillet, "Sur le choix des générateurs," 2: 158–73.

12. Roland Barthes, "The Death of the Author," in *Image/Music/Text*,
trans. Stephen Heath (New York: Hill and Wang, 1977), p. 146.

13. Robbe-Grillet identifies "the central theme of *Topologie*" as "the
raped virgin. It is really the gimmick which is in our entire civi-
lization, from Greek mythology to the popular novels you can
buy in train stations. It is truly the archetype of the novelistic and
it belongs to all classes" (interview with Vicki Mistacco in *Diacritics* 6, no. 4 [1976]: 40.

14. For a complete publication history of the texts that comprise *Topology of a Phantom City* and *Memories of the Golden Triangle*, see Bruce Morrissette's invaluable *Intertextual Assemblage in Robbe-Grillet from Topology to the Golden Triangle* (Fredericton, N.B.: York Press, 1979).

15. Ibid., pp. 76–78.

16. "Order and Disorder in Film and Fiction," trans. Bruce Morrissette, *Critical Inquiry* 4 (1977): 10–11.

17. Bruce Morrissette, for example, in speaking about Robbe-Grillet's novels and films, dissociates himself from those who believe that artists such as Robbe-Grillet are "working at the aesthetic level for the revolutionary overthrow of bourgeois values," and allies himself with "post-modern critics" for whom "generative structures isolate and protect the work of art, and by referring always back into the text (verbal or visual, or both), enable the novel or film to exist independently, aside from ideology or sociological issues, and without serving even as an instrument of propaganda for any concept of avant-garde." See his "Post-Modern Generative Fiction: Novel and Film," *Critical Inquiry* 2 (1974): 262.

18. Interview with Vicki Mistacco, *Diacritics*, p. 36.

Contributors

Anna Balakian, professor of French and comparative literature at New York University, is the author of several books, including *Surrealism: The Road to the Absolute*, *André Breton: Magus of Surrealism*, and *The Symbolist Movement*.

Ronald L. Bogue, associate professor of comparative literature at the University of Georgia, is the author of articles on Robbe-Grillet, contemporary criticism, film, and eighteenth-century aesthetics.

Betty Jean Craige, associate professor of comparative literature at the University of Georgia, is the author of *Lorca's Poet in New York*, *Selected Poems of Antonio Machado*, and *Literary Relativity*.

Arthur C. Danto, Johnsonian Professor of Philosophy at Columbia University, is the author of numerous books and articles, including *Nietzsche as Philosopher*, *Jean-Paul Sartre*, and *The Transfiguration of the Commonplace*. He was also a member of the Abstract Expressionist school of painting in New York in the 1950s.

Donald B. Kuspit, University Distinguished Professor at Rutgers University, is the author of numerous articles on painting and aesthetics, as well as the books *Dirge for a Toy Centurion* (poetry), *The Philosophical Life of the Senses*, and *Clement Greenberg: Art Critic*.

J. Hillis Miller is Frederick W. Hilles Professor of English and Comparative Literature at Yale University. He is the author of five books, including *The Disappearance of God: Five Nineteenth-Century Writers* and *Poets of Reality: Six Twentieth-Century Writers*, and a member of the Yale school of "Deconstructive Criticism."

Elliott Schwartz, professor and chairman of music at Bowdoin College, is the author of *Electronic Music: A Listener's Guide*, *Music: Ways of Listening*, and other books and articles. He is also the composer of many works performed by major orchestras and chamber ensembles throughout the United States and Europe.

Hayden White is Professor of History of Consciousness at the University of California at Santa Cruz. He is the author of numerous books, including *Metahistory: The Historical Imagination in Nineteenth-Century Europe* and *Tropics of Discourse: Essays in Cultural Criticism*.